ENGLISH GRAMMAR

THE BASICS

English Grammar: The Basics offers a clear, non-jargonistic introduction to English grammar and its place in society. Rather than taking a prescriptive approach, this book helps the reader become aware of the social implications of choices they make to use standard or non-standard (regional/dialect) forms.

Readers will consider:

- what grammar is and how it fits into the structure of language;
- how grammar functions in the school curriculum, the press, broadcasting and social media, as well as how these outlets reflect and reinforce our attitudes towards grammar;
- differences between speech and writing, as well as between formality and informality;
- major different approaches to theorising and describing grammar from important grammarians, including Noam Chomsky and Michael Halliday.

Featuring a glossary of key terms and practical tips and insights from the author's 50+ years of language teaching experience around the world, this book is for anyone who has ever found themselves questioning the 'rules' of the English language.

Michael McCarthy is Emeritus Professor of Applied Linguistics, University of Nottingham, and Adjunct Professor of Applied Linguistics, University of Limerick. He has (co-)authored and edited 54 books and is co-founder (with Ronald Carter) of the CANCODE spoken English corpus. He has lectured in 46 countries and has been involved in language teaching and applied linguistics for 55 years.

The Basics

The Basics is a highly successful series of accessible guidebooks which provide an overview of the fundamental principles of a subject area in a jargon-free and undaunting format.

Intended for students approaching a subject for the first time, the books both introduce the essentials of a subject and provide an ideal springboard for further study. With over 50 titles spanning subjects from artificial intelligence (AI) to women's studies, *The Basics* are an ideal starting point for students seeking to understand a subject area.

Each text comes with recommendations for further study and gradually introduces the complexities and nuances within a subject.

SUSTAINABILITY (SECOND EDITION)
PETER JACQUES

TRANSLATION
JULIANE HOUSE

TRANSNATIONAL LITERATURE
PAUL JAY

TOWN PLANNING
TONY HALL

WOMEN'S STUDIES (SECOND EDITION)
BONNIE G. SMITH

ENGLISH GRAMMAR
MICHAEL MCCARTHY

For a full list of titles in this series, please visit www.routledge.com/The-Basics/book-series/B

ENGLISH GRAMMAR

THE BASICS

Michael McCarthy

LONDON AND NEW YORK

First published 2021
by Routledge
2 Park Square, Milton Park, Abingdon, Oxon OX14 4RN

and by Routledge
605 Third Avenue, New York, NY 10158

Routledge is an imprint of the Taylor & Francis Group, an informa business

British Library Cataloguing-in-Publication Data
A catalogue record for this book is available from the British Library

Library of Congress Cataloging-in-Publication Data
Names: McCarthy, Michael, 1947- author.
Title: English grammar : the basics / Michael McCarthy.
Description: Abingdon, Oxon ; New York, NY : Routledge, 2021. |
Includes bibliographical references and index. |
Identifiers: LCCN 2020054550 (print) | LCCN 2020054551 (ebook) |
ISBN 9780367633660 (hardback) | ISBN 9780367633653 (paperback) |
ISBN 9780367633677 (ebook)
Subjects: LCSH: English language--Grammar. | English language--Social aspects.
Classification: LCC PE1106 .M36 2021 (print) | LCC PE1106 (ebook) |
DDC 428.2--dc23
LC record available at https://lccn.loc.gov/2020054550
LC ebook record available at https://lccn.loc.gov/2020054551

ISBN: 978-0-367-63366-0 (hbk)
ISBN: 978-0-367-63365-3 (pbk)
ISBN: 978-0-367-63367-7 (ebk)

Typeset in Bembo
by Taylor & Francis Books

For Jeanne

CONTENTS

List of figures   xiv
List of tables   xvi
Acknowledgements   xviii
Introduction to the reader   xix

1   **Everyone knows what grammar is ... don't they?**   1

A word for all seasons 1
What grammar is (and what it isn't) 2
   A rough definition 2
Traffic lights and sunrises 4
   The rules of the road 4
   Universal rules 7
Where do the conventions come from? 7
   Prescriptions for the best medicine 7
   Grammatical standard-bearers 10
Gathering more evidence 12
   I heard it on the radio 12
   At the click of a mouse 12
   Corpus evidence 13
Describing English 15

Grammar and grammars 15
Varieties of English 16
Dialects 17
Other types of variation 17
This book: What it offers and what it doesn't 18
The many-headed hydra 18
The basics 19
What else is in the chapters? 20

2   **From words to sentences**   **22**

Taking words apart 22
What's in a word? 22
Morphemes 23
Different types of morphemes 24
Morphemes and words: Building the system 25
How do words fit into grammar? 25
Words and phrases 25
Phrases and clauses 27
What is a clause? 27
Who does what? Participants and processes 28
Clauses: Different shapes, different meanings 29
Grammar and meaning 29
What sort of mood are you in? 30
Affirmative and negative 32
Clauses: Who's doing what, where, when and how? 32
Subjects and objects 32
Complements 33
A peaceful agreement: Concord 33
Adverbials: Mobility rules! 35
Are you running a business? Or just
    running? 35
Let's hear your voice: Active and passive 36
'In-between' passives 37
Clauses joining forces: Building sentences 38
What is a sentence? 38
Joining up 1: Three little words 40
Joining up 2: Subordinate clauses 40
Conditions 41

Non-finite clauses 42
Taking care of the relatives 42
Relative clauses: Common difficulties 45
Who knows what? Who said what? Reported
clauses 46
Chains or Russian dolls? 46
A place for everything: Word-order 47
Into focus 47
Sometimes at the beginning? Or at the end
maybe? 48
This section you must read 49
Scaling the heights 49
Is there life beyond the sentence? 50
Bigger links mean bigger chains 50
Linking expressions 50
Taking an axe to the sentence: Clefts 52

3 The grammar toolbox **55**

A toolbox full of words 55
What are nouns for? 55
Naming the world 55
How much coffee makes a coffee? 55
What else can nouns do? 58
Building with nouns 59
Verbs: Being, doing, happening 60
Who does what and to whom? 60
Main verbs, auxiliaries and modals 60
Auxiliary 'be': Marking aspect 61
Auxiliary 'have': Marking aspect 62
Auxiliary 'be': Marking voice 63
Aspect and voice: Using the tools together 64
Auxiliary 'do': Yes or no? 64
Auxiliary 'do' for emphasis 65
Substitute 'do' 66
Modal verbs: What's true, what's right 66
That could be true ... to a degree 66
'You must come to dinner sometime!' 67

We use small verbs as tag verbs, don't we ... or
   do we? 68
Might I ask you a question? 69
How long is a piece of string? 69
Colouring in the world: Adjectives and adverbs 70
   What's it like and how did it go? 70
   Adjectives: Telling it like it is 70
   Adverbs: How did it go? 71
   Adverbs as adverbials 72
Conclusion 73

4 The grammar toolbox continued   **75**

The other word classes 75
   Small words get everywhere 75
Pronouns 77
   Getting personal 77
   Me and my sister: Subject and object
    pronouns 78
   Reflexive pronouns: Grammatical selfies 79
   Each other and one another 80
   Is anyone out there? 80
   What it's all about: Clefts 81
   Someone or other did it 81
   The ones which matter: Relative pronouns 82
   Interrogative pronouns: What are they for? 84
   Demonstrative pronouns: This is important,
    that's not 84
Determiners 86
   Articles: Where's the cat? 87
   Interrogative determiners 89
   Possessive determiners 89
Conjunctions: Getting it together 91
   Coordinating 91
   Subordinating 92
   Correlative 92
Prepositions 93
   What are they for? 93

Prepositions: Should we leave them
    stranded? 94
No, nay, never ... 95
What about all those other small words? 96
Conclusion 97

5 Theories and thinkers   99

Putting their thinking caps on 99
It stands to reason: Logic and rules 100
Structuralism 102
Noam Chomsky and his grammar 105
    Colourless green ideas 105
    Transformations 107
    From the depths to the surface 109
Bearing everything in mind: Cognitive grammar 110
    The mind and the world 110
    Symbols and concepts 111
    Constructions 113
    Use it and never lose it 114
Out of the mind: Neo-Firthians 115
    Grammar and context 115
    Michael Halliday 117
    Functions and systems 117
    Grammar in society 119
Conclusion: Theory and theories 120

6 Word of mouth: Grammar in action   123

In a manner of speaking 123
*Speaking and writing: A grammar for every
 occasion* 126
You thinking what I'm thinking? 126
*This book, you never know what it's going to say
 next ...* 128
    Heads or tails? 128
    Pronouns, they work hard, they do 129
Mark my words 130

Taking chunks out of the language 133
We're beginning to see a pattern here 134
'I see him yesterday': Dialect grammars 136
English grammar around the world 139
Listen up and check this out! 142
Conclusion 143

7   **Grammar policy, grammar politics and grammar police**   **145**

Moral panic 145
The lost generation 147
    Grammar in the lockdown 147
    What did traditional grammar look like? 149
    Policing the grammar: Terminology 150
    (Dis-)United States 153
    Australia: Whole language or bits and
      pieces? 154
    The UK: From grammar to comprehensive 155
A balancing act 157
    Grammar makes a comeback 157
    From balance to moral panic 160
    Mr Gove and Mr Gwynne 163
Conclusion 165

8   **Grammar in the public eye**   **168**

The grammatical landscape 168
    Less or fewer? 168
Putting a (full) stop to punctuation 170
    Punctuation and grammar 170
    Full stops 171
    The rise and fall of the semi-colon 172
    Endangered species? The apostrophe 174
    Sound–spelling grammatical confusions 176
Pronouns: Not so closed after all? 178
Adverbials: Why do people get affronted? 180
Telling it like it is 181

*The linguistic landscape: Being creative with
  grammar 185*
Conclusion 186

Glossary of grammar terms   188
References   195
Index   201

FIGURES

1.1	Rules of the road	5
1.2	Laws of the universe: Sunrise	8
1.3	Extract of concordance for *end*	14
1.4	*Upon* in three registers	18
2.1	*Whom* in writing and speaking	44
2.2	Russian dolls	47
2.3	Linking in speaking and writing	52
4.1	Change in the use of *whom*	83
4.2	Interjections	97
5.1	Grammar and the chess board	103
5.2	Tree-diagram of sentence structure	107
5.3	The outer shell and the kernel	108
5.4	Imaging the sunflowers	112
5.5	Rank scale	118
5.6	Personal pronouns system: Human subjects	119
5.7	Mapping the unknown	121
6.1	'Sometimes I just sits'	137
7.1	Parsing	149
7.2	'He said his first fronted adverbial today'	164
8.1	Semi-colons	173

| 8.2 | Apostrophe use in public signs | 175 |
| 8.3 | Personal pronoun *one* | 180 |

TABLES

1.1	Three approaches to grammar	9
2.1	Types of phrases	27
2.2	Indicative mood: Declarative and interrogative clauses	30
2.3	Intransitive, transitive and di-transitive	36
2.4	Clauses or sentences?	39
2.5	Relative clauses with nouns as subject and object	43
2.6	Cohesion: Linking expressions between sentences	51
3.1	Nouns and meanings	56
3.2	Nouns as things and nouns as stuff	56
3.3	Noun phrases	60
3.4	Simple and continuous aspect	61
3.5	Present perfect and relevance to 'now'	63
3.6	Past perfect	63
3.7	Perfect aspect: Continuous form	64
3.8	Aspects and voice combined	64
3.9	Tag-types	68
3.10	Adverbs acting as adverbials	72
4.1	Top 20 most frequent words (BNC)	75
4.2	Personal pronouns	77
4.3	Interrogative pronouns	85

4.4	Articles	87
4.5	Examples of subordinating conjunctions	92
4.6	Examples of correlative conjunctions	93
6.1	Auxiliary and modal patterns	135
6.2	Concordance lines for *be* + *after* + *ing* (LCIE)	140
8.1	Emailing, texting and punctuation	172
8.2	Word-forms often confused in writing	176

ACKNOWLEDGEMENTS

Rebecca Howling for supplying the Russian nested dolls (p. 47).

David Mitchell for supplying the African chess set (p. 104).

Jake Tebbit for permission to reproduce the illustrations on pp. 121 and 164.

INTRODUCTION TO THE READER

This book gives you the basics of grammar. It is not a reference book and it is not a grammar exercise book. It does not tell you everything about English grammar. It just takes you through the basic concepts and terminology you will need if you are a schoolteacher teaching English, a teacher of English in training, a student doing your school-leaving exams or an undergraduate starting a degree course in English language or linguistics. And if you are none of these, you may find it interesting and useful in your daily life. A lot of people struggle with grammar because they never did any at school; this book, I hope, will go towards making up for that.

Knowing about grammar involves more than just knowing terminology and how to construct good sentences. It is also useful to know what theories lie behind different ways of looking at grammar, what we mean by *dialect grammar, traditional grammar* or *standard grammar*, and if you never did any grammar at school, why that was so. Knowing about grammar means appreciating that there is not just one English grammar but that there are different varieties of English grammar around the world. It also means understanding why ordinary people who are not academics have strong attitudes about grammar. This book covers all those topics, and I've tried to make them as enjoyable as possible.

By the end of the book, you will know the basics, but I hope you will want to go on and learn about grammar in the books and articles that I refer to. Grammar is a fascinating subject. I hope you enjoy reading the book as much as I enjoyed writing it.

EVERYONE KNOWS WHAT GRAMMAR IS ... DON'T THEY?

A WORD FOR ALL SEASONS

If you never studied linguistics, you might be baffled if you saw the word *morphosyntax*, a technical term known to linguists which refers to rules that explain how items are related to one another in language. But you would probably feel reasonably familiar with the word *grammar* if it cropped up in conversation. *Grammar* is also a technical term in the study of language but at the same time it is a word people use in their everyday 'language about language', as familiar as *spelling* or *punctuation*.

Most non-specialists consider grammar to be the correct application of a set of rules that are written down somewhere, passed down through the generations and taught in schools. These rules are usually thought of as logical and abstract.

However, people often confess that their own grammar is not what it should be, or that they were never taught grammar at school, or that they can't be bothered with it anyway. Often, if you pursue the question, they include their inability to spell tricky words, or not knowing when to use a comma (is it *Jim, George and Jo* or *Jim, George, and Jo?*) or an apostrophe (is it *it's* or *its?*).

People also know what upsets and irritates them about *other* people's grammar. The younger generation have let standards slip, grammar has been destroyed by texting and social media, interviewees on TV and radio start every answer to a question with 'So, ...', young people say *like* all the time, greengrocers write *banana's* instead of *bananas*, footballers say *we was robbed* instead of *we were robbed*. They may also claim that grammar is not taught properly in schools or is not taught at all. I haven't invented these grumbles – when I give talks on language to local societies, people have said them to me. People get agitated about grammar in a way that they don't get upset about physics or geography.

The word *grammar* covers different things for different people, but what they usually have in common is a belief that you can measure how well people use language against a set of rules or standards, and that going against those rules or standards is bad or wrong, or socially undesirable.

WHAT GRAMMAR IS (AND WHAT IT ISN'T)

A ROUGH DEFINITION

Here is a rough definition: English grammar is the set of items and conventions for creating acceptable English sentences. I say *rough* because we will see that there are all sorts of problems with definitions that try to be airtight. Let's unpack this one.

Items in grammar are the words and parts of words that express grammatical meanings. In English, we have items that show that something happened in the past (e.g. *was, did* or the *-ed* in *arrived*). We can indicate that something happens if certain conditions are met using words like *if* and *unless*, where something is in time or place (e.g. *at, during, in, under, here, those*), whether something is more or less possible (e.g. *may, should, must, will*), that something is specific or general (e.g. *the cat, cats*), that something is singular or plural, male or female (e.g. the *-s* in *cats, we, she*), and so on. These are all grammatical meanings carried by grammar items. Words like *chuckle, giraffe* and *silly* express a different sort of meaning; they are part of the vocabulary or **lexis** of English with which we label people, things and events in the world.

Our definition refers to the items as a **set** since they form a limited, finite group. At any point in the history of English, we can list the grammatical items that are in use and be confident that we have a complete list, a set.

Conventions are the socially agreed ways of using the items: which ones refer to who or what, how we agree to spell them and pronounce them, how we arrange them in speaking and writing (e.g. how words are put together to make phrases; the word order that makes something a question), what changes we make when we put words together (e.g. using *these* not *this* with a plural noun: *these boxes*), how we show who is doing what (*Charlie phoned Mary* is different from *Mary phoned Charlie*), whether we consider something suitable or not for the situation (is it too formal or too informal?). To qualify as conventions, the great majority of users of a language must agree that they are normal and appropriate.

Two technical terms associated with items and conventions are **morphology** (the items and what they are composed of) and **syntax** (how the items are arranged in meaningful ways).

Acceptable means something that is accepted by speakers of a language as meaningful and as the normal way of expressing something. Most of the time we don't consciously listen to one another's grammar, but we may notice when something doesn't sound or look right or seems incoherent. Perhaps it is something you can't make sense of. So, if someone writes *would a acceptable is means by accepted something that language a speakers of*, it is difficult to make any sense of it. The word order violates so many conventions English speakers have been brought up to understand and use. Rearrange the words into the order of the opening words of this paragraph and they make sense (I hope).

Sometimes, what someone says or writes contradicts what we were taught in school. This is a different sort of judgement from saying that something doesn't make sense. Someone says *Me and my sister are going to Washington*, and you remember that you were taught in school to say *My sister and I are going to Washington*. Or someone who comes from the part of Wales where I come from says *I likes pizza* and we judge them as sounding quaint or different from what we would say (e.g. *I like pizza*), or, worst of all, as less intelligent than us. Our judgements of what is acceptable might spring from a variety of different reasons or prejudices.

You may think that **English** is the least contentious word in our definition. Surely, English is the language that is not French, Japanese, Russian, Icelandic, etc.? However, English is a convenient, cover-all label for a wide range of varieties. There are the 'old' Englishes of Britain, Ireland, North America, Australia, New Zealand and so on which are different from one another, there are newer varieties of English in Asia and Africa that have developed their own vocabulary and grammar, and there are numerous ways of using English among people who just use it as a tool for professional reasons or for travel, with others who use it in that way when none of those involved would say it was their first language. And even within the English of the small island of Britain we will find a lot of variation in how people use grammar.

This book is mostly about British English because I'm British, but I will refer to the grammars of other varieties occasionally so that you don't think British grammar is special in some way.

Sentence is another slippery word. The easiest definition of a sentence is a string of words that make sense and represent a meaningful, complete idea, separated by capital letters and full stops (periods). But all sorts of combinations of words may be meaningful and represent complete ideas, and we do not use capital letters or full stops when we speak. So, we need a definition of a sentence that has internal consistency, that is systematic. We'll explore this in Chapter 2.

Lastly, the word **grammar** itself hides further complications. Grammar is something we use every day and something we study. But *a grammar* can also be a kind of book; just as we go to a dictionary to find out what words mean, we can consult a grammar (of English, Japanese, Welsh) to find out how the grammar of a language works. I have several grammars on my bookshelves. Then there is the question of what is included in a grammar, a school textbook or a reference book.

Over the centuries, grammar has included studying the origins of words, punctuation, poetic style, literary composition, as well as the conventions of how to construct sentences. Nowadays, interest has narrowed down so that we no longer consider it essential to include the origins of words or advice on literary style and composition in a grammar, but we are still interested in how grammar helps us put together meaningful texts and how the sentences in a text relate to one another.

TRAFFIC LIGHTS AND SUNRISES

THE RULES OF THE ROAD

What about *rules*? A rule is something that tells you what you are allowed to do and not allowed to do. For example, the 'rules of the road' in the UK mean you must not do certain things when driving.

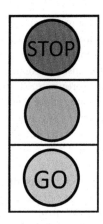

Figure 1.1 Rules of the road.

If you do what you are not allowed to do, you may be punished. A red light means STOP in the UK. In some countries it means 'stop unless you want to turn right and only if it is safe to do so'.

Grammar has some things in common with traffic lights. Just as the colours of the lights and the order in which they go on and off have meanings, the items and conventions of grammar have meanings. But the differences are important. You won't be fined or sent to prison if you disobey the grammatical conventions. People may disapprove of your grammar, form a negative impression of you or laugh at you, you may fail an examination, but only the harshest of teachers would punish you for using the wrong ending on a word. You're not likely to injure anyone by not following the conventions (unlike driving recklessly through a red traffic light), and English has no official body whose job it is to make sure we all behave grammatically.

The rules of the road can only be changed by official bodies that have the power to change them. The conventions of grammar change naturally and organically over time, and nobody can force them to change or stop them from changing. They change because societies and cultures change and because people start to use language in new ways and stop using older ways. Britain, for example, has seen successive waves of invaders and immigrants over many centuries who have left their mark on the English language, constantly renewing and enriching its grammar. The grammar we consider 'correct' today is not the same as the grammar of 600 years ago.

In this book, I try to avoid referring to rules and things that are correct or incorrect, and instead focus on what is meaningful, acceptable, normal and appropriate. This doesn't mean that my motto is 'anything goes'. Some sentences sound weird or unnatural and can't be given a coherent meaning, but I will always try to give evidence for any decision to dismiss them. So, the big question is: What is the evidence for saying something is acceptable, normal and appropriate? Grammar is not a set of abstract rules written down somewhere on tablets of stone. But we do have grammar books, and grammar syllabuses in schools, and grammar tests. Where do all these come from and why do we need them?

REFLECTION POINT

Great writers are often thought to be models of 'good', 'correct' grammar. William Shakespeare's grammar is not greatly different from English grammar today, but there are differences.

In standard English (the English taught as standard in school curriculums), it is considered incorrect to say *the most biggest city in the world*, or *your car is more bigger than ours*. These are called double **superlatives** and double **comparatives** because they seem to be illogical by unnecessarily doubling things up: we do not need *most* and *-est* together or *more* and *-er* together.

Yet Shakespeare uses forms such as *more worse, more better, most bravest, most coldest*. During Shakespeare's time, these were not considered wrong or bad grammar. One researcher of Shakespeare's works says: 'Shakespeare uses *more better* three times in his plays, and in the very large database, *Early English Books Online* (comprising a wide variety of texts from 1473–1700), *more better* occurs no fewer than 5,180 times' (retrieved from: http://wp.lancs.ac.uk/shakespearelang/2016/11/08/is-more-better-a-mistake-if-shakespeare-said-it/).

The researcher asks: Can it be a mistake if Shakespeare said it?

Over the centuries, 'double' comparatives and superlatives fell out of favour and are nowadays considered non-standard English. The grammar checker on my computer doesn't like them. However, you can still hear them in many dialects of English around the world.

UNIVERSAL RULES

The rules of the road are arbitrary, as are the conventions of grammar. There is nothing absolute in the choice of the colour green to mean 'go' – it could as easily be blue, just so long as it was clear to everyone what a blue traffic light meant. There is nothing 'logical' in the *-s* ending that makes nouns plural in English (*books, boys, girls*). Swedish makes plurals using different endings, for example, *-er*, *-ar* and *-or (books = böcker, boys = pojkar, girls = flickor)*. And if we want to say *the books, the boys, the girls* in Swedish, we say *böckerna, pojkarna, flickorna*. In English, the definite article (*the*) must come before a noun; in Swedish, it is tacked on to the end of the noun. Neither language is more logical; neither language has access to some universal law for how plurals should be formed or where the definite article should be placed.

However, there are laws that govern the universe, such as those discovered by Albert Einstein. We cannot change the universal laws of gravity, the speed of light, the behaviour of black holes or the way the sun rises and sets as the earth turns.

The laws that govern the cosmos and create sunrises are outside of us. They are universal and beyond our control. Some theories of grammar are based on the idea that there are universal forces at work in how our minds operate and that we are born hard-wired with the ability to acquire whatever language later becomes our mother tongue. Whether we end up speaking Thai, Swahili, Urdu or Arabic, there is something deep in the human mental architecture that all languages relate to. Beneath the surface of English sentences, there are universal principles that all languages share. So, some linguists believe there is a **universal grammar**. Languages may not agree on the word order in sentences or how to form plurals, but basic ideas such as subjects and verbs and objects (representing who does what) seem to be common to all languages.

WHERE DO THE CONVENTIONS COME FROM?

PRESCRIPTIONS FOR THE BEST MEDICINE

We don't know how grammar first came about, though some scientists have pondered how the earliest humans used sounds and

Figure 1.2 Laws of the universe: Sunrise.
Source: Image © M. McCarthy 2020.

learnt to put symbols together to create meanings and a basic grammar (e.g. Everett 2017).

For at least 2,000 years, grammar has been written down in manuscripts and books. In my recent book on grammar, I traced the history from Ancient Hindu culture to the present (McCarthy 2021: ch. 2). For the ancient Greeks, grammar was a companion to the study of literature and rhetoric, the art of persuasion using techniques for effective communication. Good rhetoric was something to be praised; good grammar was something to aspire to. From the beginning, the idea that there were rules and principles which, if you studied them, would make you a better communicator, was deeply entrenched.

What was important was what the *best* writers did, or at least those considered to be the best, and it was the best versus the rest. The rest, most people and the everyday use of language, were not considered suitable models for grammar.

If you only observe what great writers do and aspire to be like them, then grammar will ideally be a set of recommendations or prescriptions for what you *should* do (rather like a doctor's prescription for what medicine will be good for you). This is quite different from writing a grammar book which gives descriptions of what people *actually* do with grammar, regardless of whether it is a model for great literature, or good rhetoric or anything else. What is more, a prescription is only one step away from telling you what you should *not* do, things that are looked down upon as illogical, crude or vulgar, things which are proscribed or banned. We end up with three potential types of grammar.

Some grammars are a mixture of all three, though most have been a mix of descriptive and prescriptive over the centuries. Even the most prescriptive grammarians usually shy away from absolutely forbidding something. However, the sociolinguists James and Lesley Milroy point out that, although present-day linguists avoid prescriptive approaches and don't study prescriptivism, for the public, the need for prescriptive grammars and advice on correct usage is real (Milroy and Milroy 1999: 4).

The age of the Internet is no different, with blogs and social media postings showing the three tendencies in Table 1.1 in varying proportions. In 2010, the linguist Deborah Schaffer provided a comprehensive list of online grammar sites that showed these tendencies (Schaffer 2010). We can be sure they are still around and will be with us as long as the Internet offers a platform for venting our grammatical passions (Table 1.1).

The oldest grammars were written by hand. When printing was invented, that changed. It became possible to print large numbers of the same book, which meant that many people could read the same account of what the grammarians offered. The same model of 'good' grammar could be studied by people wherever they were, regardless of their regional or local dialect, or what a local

Table 1.1 Three approaches to grammar

descriptive	What people do; what the grammar is really like.
prescriptive	What people *should* do, based on what the 'best' writers do.
proscriptive	What people should *not* do; what is considered wrong, bad or both.

schoolteacher might say. So a **standard grammar** emerged, a grammar that could be taught in the nation's schools, a grammar to be shared among a great many people, a grammar to aspire to, one that would serve for communication in public life, in novels, newspapers, government documents, religious texts, public signs and notices, etc.

In Britain, it made economic sense for the first printed books to be in the dialect of the English East Midlands, since that dialect was familiar to the growing commercial middle classes in the south and east of England at the time. It was not that the East Midlands dialect was inherently superior to any other. No dialect is inherently superior. It is merely a historical accident that one dialect became the standard for printing, education and social advancement.

GRAMMATICAL STANDARD-BEARERS

The problem with trying to work out a standard grammar for English was not only that there were numerous dialects across Britain, but that the ways of talking about grammar were inherited from ancient Greek and Latin, especially Latin. If you describe English in terms of Latin grammar, you end up putting a square peg into a round hole. The endings on Latin words which tell you how people and things relate to one another in a sentence (the Latin **cases**) hardly exist in English. English does have some remnants of cases in words like *he/she/we* in contrast to *him/her/us*, but English depends much more on word order to show how the words in sentences relate to one another. Nonetheless, Latin had a huge influence on the writing and teaching of English grammar that lasted well into the twentieth century, and generations of students have had to struggle in grammar lessons with terminology borrowed from Latin.

Another feature of older grammars was the belief that knowing the origins of words (**etymology**) was a way of knowing how to use them. Many grammars contained sections on etymology. That tradition survived until the twentieth century, but we don't consider it important nowadays to know where words came from in order to understand and use modern English.

Older grammars often quoted great writers such as William Shakespeare and John Milton and the English version of the Christian Bible. The style of example sentences was elevated and literary. The language of the masses had no part to play in the educated standard. Even when we enter the modern era of the late nineteenth and early twentieth century, we find very stilted, formal example sentences in grammar textbooks.

We can summarise how English grammars were constructed over the centuries:

- In ancient Greece and Rome, grammar was linked to rhetoric and great writing.
- Models of grammar inherited from ancient Greece and Rome were handed down over the centuries.
- Printing made it possible to have a shared, standard grammar which schools and universities could teach.
- Terminology was taken Latin from grammar and adapted to English.
- Knowing the origins of words was part of learning grammar.
- Examples of 'good' grammar were taken from the works of great writers.
- The language of the ordinary people was generally ignored.
- Many grammars were a mix of descriptive and prescriptive approaches.

INFORMATION ADD-ON

The first English grammar written in the English language was by William Bullokar. It was published in 1586, during the reign of Queen Elizabeth I of England.

Bullokar thought English and Latin grammar had a lot in common, but he recognised that English had its own grammar and did not have the complex endings that Latin words had. He claimed his grammar would help the user achieve 'perfecter writing'.

Nowadays, most people would probably say 'more perfect' instead of 'perfecter', which shows that grammar changes.

GATHERING MORE EVIDENCE

I HEARD IT ON THE RADIO

The invention of printing meant that the works of great writers were easily available to grammarians to quote as models of good grammar. But printing also led to an increase in literacy, and a population that could read and write began to consume books and newspapers and to write and receive more and more letters. By the time we get to the end of the nineteenth century, grammarians in Britain and America were receiving personal correspondence which influenced what they put in their grammars (see the examples in McCarthy 2021: 47). Where grammarians got their evidence from was changing.

In the twentieth century, technology advanced rapidly: Sound recording, cinema, radio and television brought more factors to bear on the standardising of grammar. Radio and TV broadcasts by the BBC in the UK were delivered by people with 'posh' accents, using educated standard grammar learnt in the great British grammar schools and public schools. The linguist Jürg Schwyter shows how educated standard English and notions of correct grammar dominated the BBC for many decades (Schwyter 2016).

At the same time, it became possible to record the spoken language so that it could be studied more objectively. This opened up the possibility of describing grammar not just on the basis of the works of great literary authors. Linguists could now talk about *standard spoken English* and its grammar (Cheshire 1999; Carter 1999). The evidence could now be gathered from a wider range of sources.

AT THE CLICK OF A MOUSE

The advent of the computer was a game-changer for the study of grammar. From the 1960s onwards, linguists began to study large collections of texts stored in computers, which made it possible to look at massive amounts of English taken from many different sources. A collection of texts stored in a computer is a **corpus** (plural **corpora**). Software designed for analysing corpora enabled linguists to find out, at the click of a mouse, how common or rare certain uses of language are, and what patterns of use there are. If the texts in the corpus are annotated with information about their dates, who wrote them or spoke them, what types of texts they are (e.g. novels, news broadcasts, web pages, courtroom transcripts, conversations in shops, social media postings), then linguists can see how language is used repeatedly but also how it varies across different times, different users and different purposes and situations, i.e. different **registers**.

This kind of evidence is different from quoting the works of great writers. With a corpus, we can look at the grammar of hundreds, thousands, even millions of ordinary users of the language. This means we can obtain a more objective picture of what is common and what the conventions are which all these different users of the language are adhering to. The computer has no prejudices about 'good' and 'bad' English, it has never read a grammar book or been to school, it doesn't think Latin is special, nor does it care if something is logical or illogical. All it does is count. And what it counts helps us to see how grammar works, not how we think it works, or how we think it should work. This is proper evidence for a descriptive grammar.

In this book, I refer to corpora of British English primarily, and especially the 100 million-word British National Corpus (BNC1994) and its successor, the 10 million-word Spoken BNC2014. I also occasionally draw on other varieties of English. With the kinds of statistical evidence these and other corpora give us, we can reliably say that any sentence we are looking at follows or doesn't follow typical conventions of English grammar.

CORPUS EVIDENCE

There are three main types of evidence from corpora in this book. First, there are **frequency lists**. These are lists of words or phrases showing the most (and least) frequent items in the language, or frequency lists for individual features of grammar. Changes in frequency can tell us about changes in grammar if we see an item or a pattern of words becoming more or less frequent in sets of data collected over different periods. For instance, if we look at the texts collected in 1960–1974 in the huge 100-million-word 1994 British National Corpus (BNC1994), we find that the verb *ought* has a frequency of 130 occurrences for every one million words of text. If we look at the texts collected 1985–1993, we find this has declined to only 50 occurrences per million words. People seem to be using the word *ought* less than they used to.

Changes in frequency counts do not *explain* changes in grammar. We have to look at factors connected with social and cultural change, or influences from other parts of the English-speaking world, or the influence of school curriculums, and so on.

Corpus software allows us to produce **concordances**. A concordance brings together in one place all the different occurrences of a word or phrase in a corpus. This is very useful for observing patterns of usage.

Figure 1.3 is an extract of a concordance from the BNC1994. Each line shows a different stretch of text. The search word was *end*, and this extract of the many thousands of examples in the data shows that the phrases *in the end* and *at the end* occur. *At the end* is almost three times more common in the written texts in the data than *in the end*. *At the end* is mostly followed by *of*, and often refers to a time (*1861, December*) or a place (*the room, the corridor*). *In the end* is followed by punctuation (full stop or comma) or a break before a new part of the sentence and tells us how a series of events or arguments was finalised or resolved.

Figure 1.3 is a subset of a much bigger sample, and I can scroll up and down hundreds or thousands of examples of *end* or look at a random sample. If I want to know more about any given line in the concordance, I can click the mouse on that line and get back

he other direction. Cather"s genius,	in the end,	is to do with certainty of pace, and cer
te. But that last round of 18 pars told	in the end.	The secret of success, in my opinion, is
After all, I was brought up there and	in the end	I began to feel stifled. As for the brigh
a shadow across the french window	at the end	of the room, she felt someone catch h
g shown now in the large stockroom	at the end	of the corridor was flickering and rathe
es. The new appointments, all made	at the end	of 1861 or the beginning of 1862, besp
y stood on the green for a day or two	at the end	of April and beginning of May each yea
hile they were en route back to base	at the end	of December, there was a most puzzlin
eturning to the Centre for a day visit	at the end	of October. I had no worry about visiti
screens, designed to be taken down	at the end	of the season for service and storage.

Figure 1.3 Extract of concordance for *end*.
Source: BNC1994.

to the original text and see more of it. This is the third kind of evidence we can use to see how grammar operates: looking at longer stretches of text and making use of the information about context which is coded within the corpus (e.g. where the text comes from, when it was produced, who created it, who the speakers are, how the words or expressions I am interested in are distributed across all the texts, etc.). This sort of information is vital in building up the evidence for how words and phrases are used in different grammatical patterns and helping us to decide whether something is generally acceptable and conventional, or only used in certain types of texts, or odd or skewed in some way.

DESCRIBING ENGLISH

GRAMMAR AND GRAMMARS

English is a major world language. It is difficult to know for sure how many users it has. Millions of people have English as their first and only language, millions have it as one of two or more languages which they use in their everyday lives. The countries where English can be commonly heard alongside other languages range from India to Singapore to Kenya to The Gambia to Fiji – in other words, across the globe. Millions of others have learnt it at school and use it in international business and education. Users of English number in the hundreds of millions, whether they use English as a first or second or other language or as a **lingua franca**. Lingua franca refers to a language used by people who do not have a language in common, for example a Russian speaker might use English to do business with an Arabic speaker.

The global position which English occupies means that it is impossible to establish a one-size-fits-all version of English grammar. It is better to talk about the *grammars* of English, just as linguists nowadays refer to *World Englishes* – in fact, there is an academic journal with that title devoted to research into English in all its varieties and cultures.

VARIETIES OF ENGLISH

When we talk about *varieties* of English, we mean established national and regional forms of English that not only have their own accents, vocabulary and grammar, but which have become established as ways of expressing cultures which are not necessarily the same as the British culture of the 'old motherland' of the English language. Such varieties have their own literary traditions, for example, Indian writing in English, or the literature that has come out of African varieties of English. If we find grammatical differences in those varieties compared with British English, this tells us of the way grammar evolves to serve cultures. When some of these varieties were first described, the differences between their grammar and standard British English grammar were often looked upon as 'errors' which should be corrected, for example in early studies of the English of Nigeria (Banjo 1997). We now see them as varieties in their own right.

The Irish linguists Fiona Farr and Anne O'Keeffe show how the use of *would* as a way of saying indirectly things which are factual is a feature of Irish culture. In their corpus data, a woman calling in to a radio phone-in programme says: 'I <u>would have had</u> black hair, you know my hair <u>would be</u> brownish now but it was black in the teenage years' (Farr and O'Keeffe 2002). To the British English ear, this use of *would* is odd – why doesn't the caller just say *I <u>had</u> black hair* and *my hair <u>is</u> brownish now*? Surely the woman knows the colour of her own hair! The Irish variety of English is long-established, and its grammar reflects distinctly Irish ways of expressing things (Corrigan 2011). The verb *would* is also used in Nigerian English in a way that is different from both its standard British version and the Irish version, corresponding more to British uses of *will* (Banjo 1997). No one of these varieties is inferior or superior. They are simply different, and each variety should be considered on its own merits.

Other regions of the English-speaking world have also been investigated and show well-established local grammars that are different from the standard British variety, for example, Black South African English (Van Rooy 2013), and some shared ways of adapting and changing the ways standard British English is used, can be seen across different countries that were once part of the British Empire (Ahulu 1998).

DIALECTS

Dialects refers to regional variations within national varieties. So, in the UK we can talk of a Yorkshire dialect, in which, especially among older speakers, you may hear people calling one another *thee* instead of *you*, or referring to *yon pub* instead of *that pub*, or saying *while Thursday* rather than *until Thursday*. In Northern Ireland and parts of the United States, you may hear people saying *whenever I was a child* rather than *when I was a child*. Once again, dialect grammars are just different ways of expressing things. The problems come when dialects are dismissed as inferior or undesirable in comparison with the educated standard that is the backbone of the school curriculum. The sociolinguist Peter Trudgill, writing about the dialect of the county of Norfolk in eastern England, says:

> Standard English is the dialect which is used in books and newspapers, and in the education system, so this sort of difference has led some people to think that Norfolk grammar is 'bad grammar'. But there is nothing bad about it; it is just different. Local dialects may have lower social status than Standard English, but that does not make them 'wrong'. They just have their own, different grammars, with their own rules.
>
> (Trudgill 2016: 90)

OTHER TYPES OF VARIATION

There are other kinds of variation too. For example, the grammar used by scholars in academic writing conforms to conventions that have grown up over many years. Figure 1.4 shows the different frequencies of the preposition *upon* in three different registers of English from the BNC1994: academic writing, literary and creative writing, and general spoken English. The frequencies shown are per one million words of text.

Although it is grammatically okay to say, 'It depends upon the weather', in an informal chat with a friend it might sound a little pompous and too formal, and we might prefer *it depends <u>on</u> the weather*. Variation across registers is an important feature of grammar. The idea of registers includes formality and informality, as well as differences in the settings in which grammar is used, for

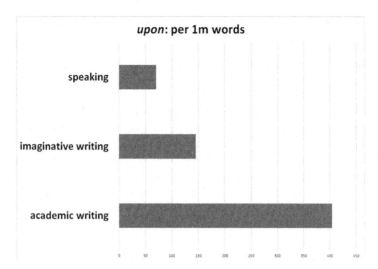

Figure 1.4 Upon in three registers.
Source: BNC1994.

example, business language, the language of religious preaching and prayer, the language of newspapers.

All of these differences mean that we have to keep a watchful eye on things before we label them as standard or non-standard, and we must be prepared to accept nuances in what is normal or acceptable rather than always looking for what is correct or incorrect. We must be alert to the fact that what may be acceptable in one situation may not be so in another. The use of dialect grammar may be fine if you are in your home dialect region chatting with friends you grew up with; it may not be such a good idea if you are writing an academic essay at university.

THIS BOOK: WHAT IT OFFERS AND WHAT IT DOESN'T

THE MANY-HEADED HYDRA

In Greek mythology, the many-headed hydra was a snake whose heads grew again as quickly as they were cut off. Grammar can be like that. To describe English grammar in all its varieties, dialects and variation across the world would mean 'cutting off heads' (eliminating variations, contradictions and other tricky issues of comparison), only to see new differences and contradictions popping up from other parts of the world and other uses of English.

In the end, this book, with its limited number of pages, and its claim to give the basics, can only scratch the surface of English grammar and all its complexities and, in most cases, if you want more detail, it will be necessary to go to one of the big reference grammars cited here and there and listed in the Further Reading sections of the chapters, or to the specific academic papers and websites in the references that deal with individual questions of grammar.

THE BASICS

This book will focus on 'the basics', the most important features and terminology of standard British English grammar, British because I am British and have devoted decades to trying to understand and teach my own grammar and I have been involved in building and researching corpora of British English. However, as an author of textbooks and courses for learners of English as a second or foreign language, I have explored American and Irish English corpora. I will quote from other varieties where it is of interest, without (I hope) breeding many-headed hydras! I want to leave you with a useful description. This book is not a complete English grammar; that would fill up a couple of thousand densely packed pages, as did the monumental grammar of Randolph Quirk, Sidney Greenbaum, Geoffrey Leech and Jan Svartvik (Quirk et al. 1985).

This book is descriptive rather than prescriptive. Its descriptions are based on British English but much of the description will apply across many varieties and registers. The examples are taken from corpora or are edited or recast based on corpus evidence and made simple and clear to illustrate a point, or else come from the hundreds of examples I've collected from reading and listening over the last 40 years and jotted down on index cards and in notebooks.

Chapters 2, 3 and 4 show how the building blocks of grammar fit together, so that by the time you come to read the rest of the book, you should be familiar with the basic terminology and will have a feel for English grammar as a system for expressing meanings rather than as a set of abstract rules. However, if you forget any of the terminology for talking about sentences after it is explained for the first time, the most basic terms can be found again in the Glossary (pp. 188–194).

Chapter 5 explores theories that show how different scholars approach grammar. Chapter 6 takes us out into the world of dialects and varieties and looks at how knowledge about everyday speaking has changed our view of grammar. Chapter 7 looks at grammar in politics and education and the place it has occupied in education systems in different countries. Chapter 8 then takes grammar out of the hands of experts and authorities and looks at it in the wide (wild) world and illustrates some of the public controversies that surround it.

Each chapter has a Further Reading section, pointing you to books or articles that will take you into a more detailed exploration of the main areas the chapter covers.

WHAT ELSE IS IN THE CHAPTERS?

You will occasionally see boxes with different types of content. They have different names:

Reflection point boxes raise questions that you might just want to stop and think about for a while. They do not have a right or wrong answer.

Information add-on boxes give extra detail or points of interest about the subject of that part of the chapter. They contain information which is not central or essential to the argument.

Corpus evidence boxes show you results of analysis using corpus software. The results are chosen to illustrate points raised in the chapter.

When you get to the end of the book, I hope you will have a better understanding of grammar and will want to learn more about it. And there is always plenty more to learn.

FURTHER READING

Swan, M. 2011. Grammar. In J. Simpson (ed.), *The Routledge Handbook of Applied Linguistics*. **London: Routledge, 557–570.**
Michael Swan, a grammarian with decades of experience and scholarship in grammatical description, gives an accessible introduction to basic concepts in grammar and discusses some of the many different approaches and their applications.

McCarthy, M. J. 2021. *Innovations and Challenges in Grammar*. **Abingdon, Oxon: Routledge.**
This book is an 'advanced level' version of the present book. Chapters 2–5 take you through the long history of grammar and how scholars have approached it, starting more than 2,000 years ago, and coming up to the twenty-first century.

Jones, C. and Waller, D. 2015. *Corpus Linguistics for Grammar. A Guide for Research*. **Abingdon, Oxon: Routledge.**
Christian Jones and Daniel Waller's book provides a clear introduction to corpora and the tools and methods used by corpus linguists. It presents specific analyses of grammatical items in different contexts and the way they form regular patterns. It has a glossary of the basic terms that corpus linguists use.

FROM WORDS TO SENTENCES

TAKING WORDS APART

WHAT'S IN A WORD?

Grammar is about the way words combine to make sentences, so we first need to understand what a word is. We could say a word is a unit of meaning with spaces before and after it. When you read this sentence, you can identify words such as *When, you, read, this, sentence* because they have spaces before and after them. However, there are no spaces when we speak, especially if we speak quickly, even if we take a breath now and then, so it is difficult to establish the boundaries of words if we only have access to the spoken form of a language. This is a problem which anthropologists wrestle with if they are trying to document newly discovered languages that have no writing systems. And sometimes, when we write in English, we have choices about where to put spaces. For example, which of these combinations of letters and spaces is acceptable?

lamp post
lamp-post
lamppost

If you enter all three versions into a search engine, you will find an enthusiastic online debate as to whether the tall poles that light our streets are one word, two words with a space, or two words with no space but a hyphen. The choice seems to depend on personal preference, or whether the difference is between different varieties of English, or what different dictionaries recommend.

INFORMATION ADD-ON

We take it for granted that modern English words all have established beginnings and endings because we are so used to spaces in writing.

Ancient Greek and Latin texts sometimes had no spaces between words, so you might have found yourself reading a text that looked a bit like this in its English equivalent:

ANCIENTLATINTEXTSOFTENHADNOSPACESBETWEENWORDS

At other times, a point symbol was used to separate words:

ANCIENT·LATIN·TEXTS·OFTEN·HAD·NO·SPACES·BETWEEN··WORDS

MORPHEMES

A good place to start is to see how far we can go in chopping words up into pieces before the pieces become meaningless. When we reach the smallest bits that still mean something, we have a unit called a **morpheme**. Here are some examples of words divided into morphemes:

keyboard	*key* – *board*
faithful	*faith* – *ful*
faithfulness	*faith* – *ful* – *ness*
started	*start* – *ed*
rewrite	*re* – *write*
quickly	*quick* – *ly*

Keyboard consists of two morphemes, but the morphemes have fused together to form a unit of meaning, in this case, the thing for typing on a computer. We don't pause to take a breath between *key* and *board*. *Faithful* has two meaningful parts: *faith,* and *-ful*, an ending meaning 'possessing that quality', as in *beautiful, careful*. Adding *–ness* in *faithfulness* makes it into a noun. The *-ed* on *started* shows that it has a past time meaning. The *re-* in *restart* tells us something is done again. The *-ly* in *quickly* refers to *how* something happened.

Some words just have one morpheme: *pepper* and *daffodil* can't be divided up any further without producing meaningless bits (e.g. *pepper* does not give us *pe-pper*, *daffodil* is not made up of meaningful bits *da – ffo – dil*). *Da-, ffo-* and *-dil* are syllables but they are not morphemes.

We can define a word as a unit of meaning consisting of one or more morphemes. Speakers of a language know what the morphemes are in their language, and they know what the common words are, even if they occasionally disagree on how to write them. As an English speaker, I know that *zugle* is not an English morpheme or an English word, even though it might mean something in another language.

REFLECTION POINT

Words are at the heart of how people see communication. Consider these common English phrases:

in other words
have a word with someone
word perfect
not a word to anyone!
a word in your ear

And the famous lines from Shakespeare's *Hamlet*, Act II Scene II:

Lord Polonius   What do you read, my lord?
Hamlet   Words, words, words.

DIFFERENT TYPES OF MORPHEMES

In the case of *started* and *quickly*, we can see two kinds of morphemes. *Start* and *quick* are words in the *vocabulary* of English. They are **lexical morphemes**. The endings *-ed* and *-ly* are part of the *grammar* of English, showing past time and manner of doing something, respectively. They are **grammatical morphemes**.

Sometimes, we add morphemes at the beginning and ends of words which change their meaning. The lexical words *start* and *perfect* can be made into *restart* (start again) and *imperfect* (the opposite of

perfect). We say that words like **restart**, **starter,** **imperfect** and *imperfect***ion**
are **derived** forms: they are built from the **base forms** of other
words. *Re-* and *im-* are **prefixes**. *Writer* (a person who writes) and
composition (the process of composing) have morphemes tacked onto
the ends of the words. These are **suffixes**. Prefixes and suffixes are
derivational morphemes.

Grammatical morphemes which can stand on their own are
grammar words. The *-ed* in *started* and *-ing* in *starting* cannot stand
on their own. They are grammatical morphemes but not grammar
words. *To, so, but, who* and *should* can all stand on their own. They
are grammar words.

In the case of units of meanings such as *lamp-post, armchair, keyboard*,
where we can see two morphemes which can themselves be lexical
words, we call these **compound words** or just **compounds**.

MORPHEMES AND WORDS: BUILDING THE SYSTEM

Words and morphemes define each other mutually. Morphemes
combine to make words, and words consist of morphemes. It is a
two-way relationship. This is what we mean by a system: its parts
operate together. We can visualise it in this way, with an arrow
pointing both up and down. The 'up' arrow means 'combine to
form'; the 'down' arrow means 'consist of':

words

morphemes

This is how we will describe the grammar in this chapter. The up
and down arrows show us that grammar is a system where all the
parts work together to create different types of meanings.

HOW DO WORDS FIT INTO GRAMMAR?

WORDS AND PHRASES

Although we may still feel that words are quite slippery animals –
we only know them because we know them – they are a good
baseline for a model of English grammar.

All words belong to **word classes**. The lexical words belong to *major* word classes (nouns, verbs, adjectives, adverbs). The grammatical words belong to *minor* word classes (e.g. prepositions, pronouns, conjunctions). We will look at the kinds of meanings the different word classes create in the next two chapters.

One of the jobs words do is to function in **phrases**. A phrase is a word or group of words that play(s) a part in forming the next, larger building-block of grammar, the **clause** (see below). These clauses are divided into phrases:

The new teacher | was feeling | very nervous.
She | sent | me | an email | this morning.
In the afternoon | the children | were given | orange juice.

Phrases are a bit like words: We recognise them because they make sense in themselves. The sentences above would read very strangely if we divided the phrases differently:

*The new | teacher was | feeling very | nervous.
*She sent me an | email this | morning.
*In | the afternoon the | children were | given orange | juice.

Linguists use the asterisk symbol (*) to indicate something that is ungrammatical or strange in some way.

Just as words can consist of one or more morphemes, phrases can consist of just one or more than one word. The term 'phrase' is a label for what the word or words are doing in the clause. This clause is divided into three phrases, each of which is only one word:

They | love | tennis.

There are different types of phrases which take their name from the names of the word classes. Table 2.1 shows some examples of the main types.

We can now extend the diagram with up and down arrows to incorporate phrases. Our system now has three levels or ranks. We can go up and down the levels as we please.

Table 2.1 Types of phrases

Type of phrase	Definition	Examples
noun phrase	a noun, a pronoun or a group of words around a noun	**music**, a black **cat**, the **car** that was stolen, **them**
verb phrase	a lexical verb or a group of verbs which includes a lexical verb	**sing**, was **working**, could **exist**, is **taking** off
adjective phrase	an adjective or group of words around an adjective	**happy**, very **ugly, good** enough
adverb phrase	an adverb or group of words around an adverb	**easily**, quite **slowly, carefully** enough
prepositional phrase	a group of words consisting of a preposition plus a noun phrase	**in** the morning, **at** school, **along** the river, **on** Sunday

phrases

↕

words

↕

morphemes

The examples in Table 2.1 show that the different types of phrases do different types of jobs in clauses. Some name and describe people and things. Some describe actions and events. Some tell us how, when, where, etc. things take place.

PHRASES AND CLAUSES

WHAT IS A CLAUSE?

The basic job which phrases do is to build **clauses**. A clause must have a verb phrase and it usually has noun phrases in various forms. It can also contain adverb and prepositional phrases. Clauses tell us about actions, states and events, who or what took part in those actions, states and events, and sometimes how, when or where things happen. Here are some clauses, divided into phrases, with the verb phrases in bold:

Run!
*Patrick | **laughed**.*
*My boss | **doesn't like** | football.*
*The new restaurant | **will open** | very soon.*
*In the end, | the old building | **was demolished**.*

Run! is a clause consisting of one verb phrase, which consists of one word, which consists of one morpheme – about as minimal as you can get.

Patrick laughed consists of a noun phrase (*Patrick*) and verb phrase (*laughed*). The phrases consist of one word each.

My boss doesn't like football has two noun phrases (*my boss / football*) and a verb phrase (*doesn't like*).

The new restaurant will open very soon has one noun phrase (*the new restaurant*), a verb phrase (*will open*) and an adverb phrase (*very soon*).

In the end, the old building was demolished consists of a prepositional phrase (*in the end*), a noun phrase (*the old building*) and a verb phrase (*was demolished*).

We see from these examples that clauses have as their most important elements verb phrases and noun phrases, with optional extras such as adverb phrases and prepositional phrases that give extra information.

WHO DOES WHAT? PARTICIPANTS AND PROCESSES

Clauses centre around verb phrases. Verbs describe actions, states and events. We can put these under the general heading of **processes**.

The noun phrases that are attached before and after the verbs are the **participants** in the clause. Participants can be people or things.

The extras, the adverb phrases and prepositional phrases that tell us about how, when, where, etc. tell us the **circumstances** surrounding what happens.

Clauses do an important job in expressing meanings about the world and the people, things, events and environments that make up human experience. Clauses are the beating heart of grammar. But they could not do their job properly without the services provided by phrases and words.

The system is now becoming complex, but it still needs arrows going up and down to express the two-way relationship of 'consist of' (down arrows) and 'combine to form' (up arrows). We can now add clauses:

The terms in our diagram and terms such as *participants, processes* and *circumstances* are mostly taken from a particular model of grammar associated with the British grammarian, Michael Halliday (see Chapter 5). Halliday's grammar is systematic and well thought-out, and it has influenced the teaching of grammar in recent years, as we shall see in Chapter 7. Although it may look a little abstract in the way we are discussing it in this chapter, Halliday's grammar is based on the idea that grammar is rooted in society.

CLAUSES: DIFFERENT SHAPES, DIFFERENT MEANINGS

GRAMMAR AND MEANING

It is wrong to think of grammar as an abstract set of rules that are sent to torment us and which we simply have to learn in order to be considered 'correct' and as upstanding, educated members of society. The way English grammar has coalesced into a system reflects the way we organise the world and our experiences in it. Grammar has meaning. And just as words have different meanings that we know or look up in a dictionary, clauses have different meanings depending on what kinds of phrases we find in them and how the phrases are arranged.

Looking at grammar in this way is from a functional perspective. The way we organise meaning in our sentences and texts depends on the functions of the elements we choose to put into them.

Grammar is not a catalogue of rules; it is a system of socially agreed conventional choices for making meaning.

WHAT SORT OF MOOD ARE YOU IN?

There are three types of meanings in clauses that are called **moods**. The clauses *I love pasta* and *Do you love pasta too?* are in the **indicative** mood, because they deal with facts and things that are known about the world. However, our two examples about pasta state a fact and ask a question about a fact; we can sub-divide the indicative into **declarative** and **interrogative**, which, for convenience, we often call statements and questions, respectively. Table 2.2 shows some more examples.

We can see in Table 2.2 that changing something from a statement to a question involves changes to the word order. *She is* becomes *is she, you can* becomes *can you*. The words are inverted.

Run! is not about facts; it is an order to someone to do something. Other examples are *give me a few minutes, look at these flowers, listen to this*. This is the **imperative** mood. In English, the imperative mood just uses the **base form** of the verb (the form without any extra endings), regardless of whether we are ordering one person or more than one person to do something.

The third mood is the **subjunctive** mood. It is about things which are unreal or hypothetical. You may remember struggling with it if you learnt French or Spanish at school. In Spanish, you have to use a special set of verb endings if you want to translate the bold verbs in these clauses: *I want you **to stay** with me; If I **knew** the answer, I would tell you*. The verbs in bold refer to events which are not (yet) a reality.

Table 2.2 Indicative mood: Declarative and interrogative clauses

Indicative mood	
Declarative (statements)	*Interrogative (questions)*
She is my cousin.	Is she your cousin?
You can order the tickets online.	Can you order the tickets online?
The new phone costs more than $900.	Does the new phone cost more than $900?

The English subjunctive mood is not very common and, generally, we only find it in rather formal speaking and writing. It is most often used in the expression *if I were you* ..., and even then, many people say *if I was you* when they are speaking informally.

We also find the subjunctive in expressions starting with *were* and including a verb in the *to*-infinitive form, such as:

Were *it **to prove** necessary, we could fit a new pump.*
Were *the government **to agree**, this would represent a major change.*

This use of *were* is not very common in informal, everyday speaking, but it is considered to be an important piece of grammar in the English language requirements of the National Curriculum for England, to be taught to children aged 10–11.

CORPUS EVIDENCE

The British National Corpus (BNC1994) shows that the subjunctive construction with *were* as in *were it to be necessary* is almost twice as frequent in writing as in speaking.

If I was you is ten times more frequent in speaking than in writing. *If I were you* is by far the more common form in writing.

There is another use of the subjunctive to express ideas that are not (yet) a reality. It involves verbs such as *require, demand, insist*, the corresponding nouns *requirement, demand, insistence* and some adjectives (e.g. *important, essential, desirable*). In these cases, in very formal English, the verb that follows is always in the base form:

*The company insists that he **return** at once to the UK (less formal: that he should return).*
*The school considers it important that every pupil **learn** at least one musical instrument.*

This subjunctive form is more commonly used in American English than in British English.

AFFIRMATIVE AND NEGATIVE

All three moods in the previous section can express things in terms of **affirmative** ('positive') and **negative**:

	affirmative	**negative**
indicative	*She likes ice-cream.*	*She doesn't like ice-cream.*
imperative	*Run!*	*Don't run!*
subjunctive	*I insist that he be allowed in.*	*I insist that he not be allowed in.*

CLAUSES: WHO'S DOING WHAT, WHERE, WHEN AND HOW?

SUBJECTS AND OBJECTS

Clauses give information about participants and they can also give information about circumstances. Some participants are the 'doers' of actions. Some participants are on the receiving end of actions. The main 'doer' is the **subject**; the main 'recipient' is the **object**. We can label clauses with letters to indicate subject (S), verb (V) and object (O), as in these examples:

```
   S         V              O
Charlie | bought | a bunch of flowers.
      S           V
The children | laughed.
```

Sometimes there are two participants on the receiving end of an action. We could add another participant to our sentence about Charlie and the flowers:

Charlie bought his neighbour a bunch of flowers.

The neighbour is the receiver or final destination of the flowers; the flowers are the things that Charlie buys. The neighbour is the **indirect object** (IO). The flowers are the **direct object** (DO). In English, the indirect object comes before the direct object.

```
   S       V          IO              DO
Charlie | bought | his neighbour | a bunch of flowers.
```

We can also express this same relationship using a prepositional phrase (underlined) instead of an indirect object:

Charlie bought a bunch of flowers <u>for his neighbour</u>.

If we add information about the circumstances surrounding the event to the clause, we call these **adverbials** (A). Some grammars call them *adjuncts*:

A	S	V	IO	DO	A

Yesterday | Charlie | bought | his neighbour | a bunch of flowers | for her birthday.

Adverbials are usually adverb phrases (e.g. *yesterday, most surprisingly*) or prepositional phrases (e.g. *for her birthday, in a hurry*).

Some grammars call everything after the subject the predicate. The predicate gives all the necessary information about what the subject did:

S   predicate ──────────────────►

Charlie | bought a bunch of flowers for his neighbour.

COMPLEMENTS

Some verbs do not express actions but describe states, such as being, feeling, looking, tasting, becoming. We say that these verbs take a **complement** (C), which is usually an adjective phrase or a noun phrase:

S   V   C
Evelyn | is | an engineer.
S   V   C
It | tastes | nice.
S   V   C   A
Joe | seems | very happy | lately.
   S   V   O   C
Her remarks | made | me | angry.

A PEACEFUL AGREEMENT: CONCORD

A 'concord' between countries is a state of agreement and peace. There is also a type of agreement that happens in clauses. For example, if the subject is plural, then the verb must have a plural ending. This is called subject-verb **concord** or subject-verb **agreement**:

*The bus **is** on time.*
*The bus**es** **are** always late.*

Sometimes we can think of the subject in two different ways, either as a single or collective idea, or as a number of individuals:

*The government **is** planning to borrow 200 billion dollars over the next two years (the government as a single collective body).*
*The government **are** particularly keen to encourage small enterprises (the government as a number of individuals).*

When the noun phrase is complex and contains within itself another noun, speakers often take the cue for concord from the nearest noun rather than the main noun:

*The value of these measures **are** often overlooked.*

Standard English grammar would require:

*The **value** of these measures **is** often overlooked.*

Value is the main noun, and it is singular, so the verb should be singular if we base our decision on the standard convention. If we base our decision on other factors, such as seeing a noun as a collective or as a set of individuals, or being influenced by a nearby noun, then this is **psychological concord**. Here is an example from BBC radio:

The unity of the 27 member states are important.

An advertisement for a book on animals on the *New Scientist* magazine website asks:

WHICH IS BETTER, CATS OR DOGS?
(https://shop.newscientist.com/collections/latest/products/
cats-vs-dogs?variant=32862229397601)

Standard grammatical concord requires *Which **are** better, cats or dogs?* *Which **is*** suggests the writer is thinking of the choice between one idea (owning a cat) and another (owning a dog) and is perfectly natural-sounding.

Psychological concord often passes unnoticed in the stream of speech, but it may be more noticeable in a piece of formal writing.

ADVERBIALS: MOBILITY RULES!

In English statements (declaratives), subjects come before verbs, verbs come before objects and complements, indirect objects come before direct objects. In questions (interrogatives), auxiliary verbs come before the subject, the subject still comes before the main (lexical) verb, and so on. Adverbials are much more mobile. Here are some examples of possible places where the adverb *tomorrow* and the prepositional phrase *in the future* could be used:

***Tomorrow**, the government will reveal its budget for the coming year.*
*The government will **tomorrow** reveal its budget for the coming year.*
*The government will reveal its budget for the coming year **tomorrow**.*
*The government will reveal its budget **tomorrow** for the coming year.*
***In the future**, humans might colonise other planets.*
*Humans might, **in the future**, colonise other planets.*
*Humans might colonise other planets **in the future**.*

These are questions of style and emphasis. Putting the adverbial first, called a **fronted adverbial**, is a way of focussing on it. Putting it between the auxiliary verb (*will, might*) and the lexical verb (*reveal, colonise*), often sounds more formal.

ARE YOU RUNNING A BUSINESS? OR JUST RUNNING?

In the earlier examples, we had various numbers of participants:

<u>The children</u> laughed.	one participant
<u>Charlie</u> bought <u>a bunch of flowers</u>.	two participants
<u>Charlie</u> bought <u>his neighbour some flowers</u>.	three participants

How many participants there are and how they relate to one another is a question of **transitivity**. Verbs that usually take an object are called **transitive** verbs. Verbs that do not take an object are called **intransitive** verbs. These are just convenient labels. In fact, it is more accurate to talk about verbs being used transitively or intransitively. From the title of this section, we can see that some verbs can be used either way.

Verbs which can have two objects, an indirect one and a direct one, for example, *bring, give, send, take*, are called **di-transitive**. Table 2.3 gives examples of verbs use in these different types of transitivity.

LET'S HEAR YOUR VOICE: ACTIVE AND PASSIVE

So far, the clauses in our examples have been simple and straight-forward. In all cases, the subject has been the person or thing 'doing' something or experiencing a state or a feeling. Objects have all been people and things on the receiving end. The examples have all been **active voice** clauses. Active voice clauses are clauses where the 'doer' and the subject coincide.

But what about these clauses?

The flowers were bought at the local market.
Exams are usually taken in the autumn.
That email was sent in error.
She has been arrested.

The subjects of these clauses are *the flowers, exams, that email* and *she*, respectively. They are the subjects because they are in the position occupied by subjects. But these subjects are not 'doing' anything; they

Table 2.3 Intransitive, transitive and di-transitive

	Subject	*Verb*	*Indirect object*	*Direct object*
intransitive	My phone People	rang. were complaining.		
transitive	They We	boarded sold		the train. our house.
di-transitive	I William	sent gave	her everyone	an email. a present.

are on the receiving end of the doing. *Psychologically*, they are still the 'object' of the action. The people who bought the flowers, take the exams, sent the email, or arrested the woman are not mentioned. The examples are all **passive voice** clauses. The passive voice uses the psychological object as the grammatical subject.

The passive is constructed with the verb *be* and the past participle. The **past participle** is the third part of a verb when we say its three parts (present, past and past participle), as in *look, looked, looked; speak, spoke, spoken; drink, drank, drunk; sit, sat, sat*.

So we make a distinction between the **grammatical subject** (*the flowers, exams, that email, she*) and the psychological or 'real' subject (whoever bought the flowers, took the exams, sent the email, arrested the person). We can call this real subject the **agent**, and the agent is either not mentioned or can be mentioned using *by*, as in:

The building was designed by a famous architect.
She was arrested by two plain-clothes police officers.
The controversial email was sent by a new member of staff.

If the agent is mentioned, we call these **by-passives**; if not, we call them **agentless** passives.

We can also make passive voice clauses where the grammatical subject is the indirect recipient. These involve verbs which are di-transitive (e.g. *give, send*):

I was given a lovely scarf for my birthday.
She was awarded damages of £100,000.

In informal language, we can make the passive voice with *get* instead of *be*:

She got arrested by two plain-clothes police officers.
My brother's bike got stolen.
I got promoted last year.

'IN-BETWEEN' PASSIVES

English has various ways of expressing passive-type meanings. So far, we have just considered the *be*-passive and the alternative *get*-passive. The following sentences also have passive meanings, in that the grammatical subject is not the same as the agent:

I **had** *my flat* **decorated**.
I **had** *my watch* **stolen** *in the dressing room at the gym*.

If I have my flat decorated, it normally means I have hired someone to do it. If I have my watch stolen, it usually means I had no part in the theft, unless I am involved in an insurance fraud! Context determines how we interpret such sentences.

CORPUS EVIDENCE

In 1999, Ron Carter and I published the results of research we did into the *get*-passive in a corpus of 1.5 million words of everyday conversations.

We found 139 *get*-passives of the type *get killed, get locked out, get criticised*. No fewer than 124 of them were in contexts which were negative or problematic from the speaker's point of view (Carter and McCarthy 1999).

Although there are exceptions (people *get promoted, get chosen* for a team, etc.), it seems that the *get*-passive is particularly attracted to bad news!

CLAUSES JOINING FORCES: BUILDING SENTENCES

WHAT IS A SENTENCE?

There are a number of ways that clauses can get together to create sentences. First, we need to establish what a sentence is.

As with words, it is easier to define a sentence in writing because they start with a capital letter and end with a full stop (period). In speaking, we don't have capital letters and full stops.

Instead, we define a sentence as a unit of grammar which consists of at least one **main clause**. A main clause is a clause which can stand on its own and still make sense – it does not need anything to be attached to it to be complete. Main clauses are sometimes called *independent* clauses for this reason. In Table 2.4, all the items are clauses (they contain verb phrases) but only the ticked ones (✓) can be main clauses. The ones with crosses (X) seem to be hanging in the air. They need something else to complete them. That is why they have three dots (…) after them:

Table 2.4 Clauses or sentences?

Clause	Sentence?
Ireland is a beautiful country	✓
When I get home …	X
Glancing out of the window …	X
We always have cereal for breakfast	✓
To turn the computer on …	X
Does he work for the government?	✓
Shut the door!	✓
Looked at another way …	X
As the plane was taking off …	X

The clauses with X in Table 2.4 all need to be joined to main clauses before they can become complete sentences. Once we add main clauses (underlined), we have good sentences:

When I get home, <u>I'll give you a call</u>.
Glancing out of the window, <u>she saw a big bird of prey</u>.
<u>Press that switch there</u> to turn the computer on.
Looked at another way, <u>this could solve two problems for us</u>.
As the plane was taking off, <u>I suddenly felt very sad</u>.

The clauses which needed main clauses to be part of complete sentences are **subordinate** clauses. Subordinate clauses cannot stand on their own; they need to be attached to main clauses to make complete sense.

All sentences must have at least one main clause. They can have more than one main clause, and they often have subordinate clauses as well, but they must have one main clause. If they have more than one clause, there are various ways in which the clauses can be joined.

JOINING UP 1: THREE LITTLE WORDS

The simplest way of putting clauses together is joining them with three very common words: *and, but* and *or*. These three words are conjunctions (they 'con-join' things). They join clauses by coordinating them, putting them together like links in a chain. They are **coordinating conjunctions**. This way of linking clauses to one another is coordination:

*He plays football **and** manages a local team.*
*When you're at the shops, **and** if you have time, can you get some flour?*
*The teacher's nice **but** she's very strict.*
*When you see her, **but** only if you get an opportunity, can you mention it to her?*
*We could fly **or** we could take the train.*
*If your flight is late **or** if it is cancelled, let me know at once.*

As we can see from these examples, we can coordinate two main clauses or two subordinate clauses.

Because the conjunctions *coordinate* clauses, they join clauses which have the same pattern. The following combinations are not well-formed English sentences because the speaker is trying to combine two unequal patterns. The asterisk (*) means there is something not typical or odd in the sentence:

*She plays the guitar and joining a rock band.
*We wanted to go to the beach but if it was raining.

Thinking of coordination like the links in a chain can be helpful. Trying to join links of different sizes can be tricky.

JOINING UP 2: SUBORDINATE CLAUSES

There are two main types of subordinate clauses. The first type uses **subordinators**. These are words like *when, if, as, because, since, unless, before, after*. In these examples, the subordinate clauses are underlined, and the subordinators are in bold.

__After__ I left school, I got a job as a van-driver.
*I took it back to the shop **because** it was too big for me.*

*You can, **if you wish**, defer the examination till next year.*
***Before** you close that file, can you save it on to this memory stick?*
*He's been really happy **since he got that new job**.*
*Does she always close her eyes **when she sings**?*

We see in these examples that the subordinate clauses can come before the main clause, after it or in the middle of it (*you can, if you wish, defer* ...). This last option, interrupting the main clause, is usually rather formal. We can also see that when the subordinate clause comes first or in the middle of the main clause, we separate it off with commas. If it comes after the main clause, we don't need a comma.

CONDITIONS

Clauses with *if* and *unless* are **conditional** clauses: They state the conditions for something to happen. They can refer either to things which always happen under certain conditions as well as things which will only be real if the conditions are met. The 'always real' ones are relatively straightforward:

If I spend too long reading, I get a headache. (always the case)
Unless you have a heavy goods vehicle licence, you can't drive a lorry. (always the case)

The 'unreal' ones use modal verbs such as *will, could, would* in the main clause:

*If I won the lottery, I **could** give up my job.*
*She **would** have come tonight if she had known you were going to be there.*

In this last type, with *had* in the conditional clause, speakers often 'double up' the verb *have*. In this extract from the BNC1994, the speaker is commenting on the unsatisfactory lay-out of the tables at a meeting:

I didn't realize it would be quite as tricky as this. If it **had have** been, if we'd have known, we'd have pulled the tables further, pulled the tables further across that way.

(BNC1994 HYG)

A similar example comes from an interview in a magazine:

> I mean, I'm glad I've got children now, but if I **hadn't have** had them,
> I wouldn't know they were good.
>
> (*The Times Magazine* 24 October 2020: 21)

In both these examples, the second *have* in bold is not strictly speaking necessary, but it is so common that people do not notice it or consider it unacceptable.

NON-FINITE CLAUSES

Another type of clause combination is when a **non-finite clause** is joined to a main clause. Non-finite clauses are clauses where the verb has no subject and is in the *to*-form, the *-ing* form or the *-ed* form:

__To__ protect your identity, change your passwords frequently.
Mak__ing__ my way down the hill, I came into the village.
Encourag__ed__ by her colleagues, Laura applied for the job.

In these sentences, we know who the subject is by looking at the main clause. 'You' will be the one to change your passwords, 'I' made my way down the hill and 'Laura' was encouraged by her colleagues.

Sometimes, clauses can be introduced by a preposition with an *-ing* form. These operate in a similar way:

__After__ seeing that documentary, I never want to swim in the sea again.
__By__ studying every evening for a month, she passed the exam second time around.
__In__ conducting the review, the government took into account regional differences.

TAKING CARE OF THE RELATIVES

Sometimes, clauses are attached to nouns. These are called **relative** clauses. In these examples, the noun phrases are underlined, and the relative clauses are in bold.

*At school, <u>the subject **I liked best**</u> was geography.*
*<u>A car **which was parked nearby**</u> was used as the getaway vehicle.*
*The prize is given every year to <u>the student **who gets the highest marks**</u>.*
*<u>The athlete **whom I admire most**</u> is Usain Bolt.*
*<u>The woman **I spoke to**</u> had a Russian accent.*

In the first example, we could say 'the subject *that* I liked best' or 'the subject which I liked best'. *That* could be used in the second one: 'a car *that* was parked nearby'. In the last example, if we were being very formal, we could say 'the woman *to whom* I spoke'.

Relative clauses start with *who* (for people), *which* (for things), *that* (people or things). *Whom* is used in very formal situations. Where there is no word introducing the clause, we will use the symbol Ø, meaning 'zero'. Which word we choose depends on whether the noun is the subject or object of the verb in the relative clause. Table 2.5 shows how this works. In the first examples with *who, the athlete* wins, so he/she is the subject, while I am the one who admires (I am the subject) and the athlete is the object of my admiration.

There is most flexibility when the noun is the object. We cannot use the Ø relative or *whom* when the noun is the subject of the verb.

Who, which, that and *whom* are **relative pronouns**. *Whose* is also a relative pronoun; it indicates possession:

Table 2.5 Relative clauses with nouns as subject and object

	Noun as subject	Noun as object
who	the athlete who won the race	the athlete who I admire most
which	a car which was parked nearby	the first car which I owned
that	the athlete that won the race	the first car that I owned
Ø		the athlete I admire most the first car I owned
whom		the athlete whom I admire most

*The couple **whose** daughter won the gold medal live next door to me.*

Verbs which include prepositions can be used in two ways:

*The woman **I spoke to** had an American accent.*
*The woman **to whom I spoke** had an American accent.*

The second version is very formal. Some traditionalists prefer it because if we say *the woman I spoke **to***, or *the friend I came **with***, or *the shop I'm looking **for***, the prepositions seem to be dangling at the end of their clauses. These are called **stranded prepositions**, and very traditional grammarians believe we should not end clauses with prepositions. However, educated speakers do this all the time and it is perfectly acceptable. *Whom* is much more common in writing than in speaking. Figure 2.1 is based on the written and spoken versions of the BNC.

If the information in the relative clause is essential to identify who or what we are talking about, then it is a **defining** relative clause. If the information is extra and not essential, it is a **non-defining** relative

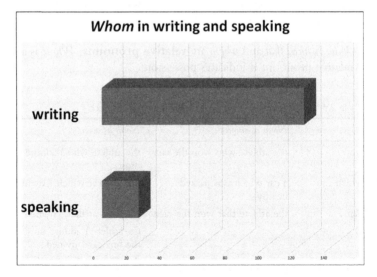

Figure 2.1 Whom in writing and speaking.

clause. Defining clauses are used without commas; non-defining ones are separated by commas:

My cousin who lives in Australia is a farmer. (defining, no comma: Essential information to identify which of my cousins I am talking about)
My father, who left school at 15, worked all his life as a miner. (non-defining, with commas: The relative clause does not define or specify which father I am talking about)
One city which I would love to visit is Prague. (defining, no comma: Essential information to identify which city I am talking about)
Latvia, which is a member of the European Union, has a population of 1.8 million. (non-defining, with commas: The relative clause does not define or specify 'which Latvia?' or which country I am talking about)

One more type of relative clause is when a *which*-clause refers to or comments on a whole clause or sentence. These are **sentential** relative clauses:

He passed all his exams, which made his parents very happy indeed.

It is the whole event of their son passing his exams which delights the parents.

RELATIVE CLAUSES: COMMON DIFFICULTIES

As a teacher, over many years I've noticed problems that crop up time after time with relative clauses in students' writing. Sometimes, people are tempted to use a comma after a defining relative clause, especially when the noun phrase is the subject of the main clause, probably because the whole phrase often feels rather long, for example:

★The speaker who made the longest speech in the end-of-term debate, spoke for a whole hour.

The asterisk (★) means there is something not quite right – in this case it's the comma after *debate*. The whole noun phrase *the speaker who made the longest speech in the end-of-term debate* is the subject of the verb *spoke*. We do not use a comma between a subject and its verb.

Another problem is confusing *whose* and *who's*. *Who's* is short for *who is* or *who has*; *whose* is the relative pronoun:

Who's coming to dinner tonight? (Who is coming …?)
Who's taken my coffee mug? (Who has taken …?)
*He's the man **whose** photo was in the newspaper the other day.* (relative pronoun)

WHO KNOWS WHAT? WHO SAID WHAT? REPORTED CLAUSES

Clauses which are the objects of verbs such as *say, know, under-stand, believe, mention, state, comment, prove*, etc. are **reported clauses**. They 'report' or tell what people know, understand, say, etc. We can often leave out *that* at the beginning of the reported clause:

The police knew (that) she was lying.
This proves (that) we were right all along.
I know what you mean.
Did he mention where he was going?

CHAINS OR RUSSIAN DOLLS?

Earlier in this chapter, we suggested the image of the links in a chain was a good way of thinking of coordination (connections with *and, but, or*). However, relative clauses and reported clauses show that clauses can live inside phrases and inside other clauses, respectively. They are more like Russian 'nesting' dolls: We open up a large doll and find a smaller bit inside which is itself a doll.

Grammar has both types of relationship – 'chaining' and 'nesting' (or 'embedding'); that is why it can sometimes seem very complex and difficult to unravel.

Figure 2.2 Russian dolls.
Source: Image © M. J. McCarthy 2020.

A PLACE FOR EVERYTHING: WORD-ORDER

INTO FOCUS

Meaning in English can also be affected by word-order. A simple analogy is taking a photograph. You may want to take a general, sharp-focus shot of a landscape or you may wish to focus on somebody's face and blur the background. Grammar allows us to create sharper focus in selected parts of a clause or sentence to refine our message and to make clear to the listener/reader what we want to focus on. One way this can be done is by manipulating the word-order. We have seen, for example, how the passive voice can put the focus on the 'receiver' of an action by making the receiver the grammatical subject.

In English, some word-orders are quite fixed, with little opportunity to change them. For example, simple statements have the word order subject – verb – object. This is not so in all languages: Spanish, for example, can make statements with the subject after the verb. Changing around the word order of a simple statement in English can fundamentally change the meaning: *Harry ate the chicken* is a banal event; *the chicken ate Harry* is hot news!

However, with certain types of phrase, English offers different possibilities for what we call **information focus**. This happens with adverbials, which can be fronted for emphasis. Sometimes, the convention is to invert the verb and the subject using an auxiliary verb in the same way as we would in a question, especially with negative adverbials.

<u>*Never*</u> **had we seen** *such a huge amount of snow in one day.*

In more formal and literary styles, we find inversions after adverbs like *then* and *seldom*:

He began work as a chemist in a paint factory. Then **came the meeting** *with the woman whom he was to marry,* ... (BNC1994 AO5)
Seldom **has a team been** *so fired up prior to a major match,* ... (BNC1994 K2D)

This type of fronting with inversion creates a greater focus on the adverbials.

SOMETIMES AT THE BEGINNING? OR AT THE END MAYBE?

Some adverbials have a preferred or most typical position, what linguists call the **unmarked** position. Focus can then be put on them by moving them to other positions. For example, adverbials expressing frequency (e.g. *often, sometimes, usually, always*) have their unmarked position between the subject and main verb, or after the first auxiliary or modal verb:

I **usually** *have toast for breakfast.*
They **sometimes** *park outside our house.*

By moving the adverbs to a less typical position, what linguists call a **marked** position, we can put a greater focus on the adverb:

Usually *I have toast for breakfast.*
I have toast **usually** *for breakfast.*

THIS SECTION YOU MUST READ

The title of this section has put the object in first position, before the subject, giving us a word order of O–S–V: Object – Subject – Verb. This enables emphasis to be put onto the object *this section*, perhaps for contrast or just to highlight something important or newsworthy. The unmarked version of the title (*you must read this section*) puts far less emphasis on the object.

CORPUS EVIDENCE

In these examples from the BNC1994, the objects are underlined.

That question I think I can answer. (BNC1994 FP8)
Inside the hall he removed his cap and dropped his bag. His cap he put on a vacant coat hook. His bag he left where it fell. (BNC1994 HD7)
My binoculars I wore round my neck at the ready for all those puffins, razor bills and guillemots I expected to see on the way over. (BNC1994 F9H)

SCALING THE HEIGHTS

We have now come to the point where we can complete our description of the grammatical system. We can add sentences to the diagram:

sentences

↕

clauses

↕

phrases

↕

words

↕

morphemes

Morphemes combine to make words, words combine to make phrases, phrases combine to make clauses and clauses combine to make sentences. We can also work our way down the diagram and say sentences consist of clauses, clauses consist of phrases, and so on.

IS THERE LIFE BEYOND THE SENTENCE?

In this chapter, we have built a system where sentences consist of clauses, clauses consist of phrases, phrases consist of words and words consist of morphemes. Can we subdivide morphemes just as physicists split atoms? And when we string sentences together to form paragraphs, essays, or any other kinds of texts, do we enter a world of super- or macro-grammar? Or can we just forget grammar and talk about something a bit more nebulous, such as 'style' or 'composition'?

At the smallest end of the grammar, morphemes, we can often chop morphemes up into syllables, but then we are into the worlds of sounds and spellings, that is to say, the **phonology** (sounds) and **orthography** (writing system) of the language.

At the top end of the system, beyond the sentence, grammarians can make some statements which are useful for understanding ways in which sentences can connect with one another to build coherent and meaningful texts, and this area of study is sometimes called **discourse grammar**.

BIGGER LINKS MEAN BIGGER CHAINS

LINKING EXPRESSIONS

Sentences can be related to one another through linking expressions. These include words like *however, therefore, consequently, next, subsequently*, and phrases like *as a result, in addition, on the other hand*. They most often come at the beginning of the second sentence, but they can be used elsewhere, depending on how formal the style is. Linking expressions are important because they make explicit for the reader or listener how the writer or speaker intends the sentences to be understood in relation to each other. They create **coherence** between sentences. The expressions themselves are called **cohesive devices**, and the different types of connections they create come under the general heading of **cohesion**.

There are four main types of linking expressions. They signal different types of logical relationships between sentences, as shown in Table 2.6.

Figure 2.3 shows how some linking expressions have very different frequencies in writing compared with speaking.

Another example is *perhaps*, which is over three times more frequent in writing than in speaking. On the other hand, *maybe*, close in meaning to *perhaps*, is over ten times more frequent in everyday spoken language than in writing.

These figures do matter, for they tell us how particular choices are likely to be perceived. Use *maybe* in a formal academic essay and you run the risk of being heard as too informal. Use *subsequently* in an informal, friendly chat and your friends might find you rather pompous.

Table 2.6 Cohesion: Linking expressions between sentences

Type	Example
Adding or additive	Financial guarantees are essential. **Furthermore**, you must show evidence of being debt-free for at least five years.
	She invested money on the stock market. **In addition**, she bought a city-centre apartment and rented it out.
Adversative or opposing/contrasting	They had offended everyone. **Yet** they didn't seem to realise it.
	He's not much of a singer. **On the other hand**, he plays the piano reasonably well.
Time	He left university in 2015. He **subsequently** tried a number of different jobs but never found the right one.
	First, download the app. **Next**, when prompted, click 'install'. **Then** enter your personal details.
Cause and effect	The hurricane damaged power lines. Many homes were left without electricity **as a result**.
	The small print covers the manufacturer against a wide range of potential problems. **Consequently**, the client has very few rights.

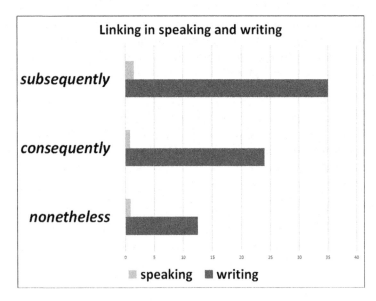

Figure 2.3 Linking in speaking and writing.

TAKING AN AXE TO THE SENTENCE: CLEFTS

The word *cleft* is the past participle of the verb *cleave* (*cleave – clove – cleft*), which means to split something with a heavy blow, for example with an axe. We can do this, metaphorically speaking, with sentences. In the following sentences, in the second of each pair (b), we have kept the same basic meaning but split the sentence into two clauses, each with its own verb (in bold):

a   *Charlie finally **solved** the mystery.*
b   *It **was** Charlie who finally **solved** the mystery.*
c   *We now **need** someone with good people skills.*
d   *What we **need** now **is** someone with good people skills.*

The (b) sentences are called **cleft sentences**. The sentence beginning with *it* is an **it-cleft** and the sentence beginning with *what* is a **wh-cleft**.

We might use a cleft to create emphasis, or to make the cleft sentence stand out in some way from the sentences around it.

Often, a *wh*-cleft sentence in a paragraph is a good indication that that sentence is the most important one for the reader to focus on.

In this paragraph from my previous book on grammar, I am talking about the types of examples found in a very popular grammar book published in 1898. I wanted to make the point that the spread of English around the world had a long-lasting effect. I used a *wh*-cleft sentence to highlight my argument:

> The user is also reminded that the English language has spread beyond its native homeland to North America, Australia, New Zealand, India, Burma and South Africa, 'and is beginning to be spoken by the natives in Egypt and in several parts of China and Japan' (p. 304). **What we should take from these examples is a picture of the increasingly important role of English** in a vast empire and in the world as a whole – a paternalistic enterprise that would see particular forms of language experience and approaches to grammar spread across the globe to become entrenched for a long time.
>
> (McCarthy 2021: 38)

This use of the *wh*-cleft is an example of discourse grammar: The grammar of the sentence is sensitive to the needs of the paragraph, not vice-versa.

In this chapter we have looked at how words are strung together in units of different sizes and how the units relate to one another to build a system. In the next chapter, we consider the words of English as a toolbox full of tools that enable us to create a wide range of different meanings.

FURTHER READING

Downing, A. 2015. *English Grammar: A University Course*. 3rd edition. Abingdon, Oxon: Routledge.
Angela Downing takes a functional approach, always concerned with how grammar creates meanings rather than seeing grammar as a set of abstract rules. The book is full of natural examples, including ones taken from corpora, and covers British and American sources.

Eastwood, J. 1994. *Oxford Guide to English Grammar*. **Oxford: Oxford University Press.**

Sections 1–13 of John Eastwood's book will give you further detail on the areas covered in this chapter. Section 51 on Emphasis is also relevant. Each section shows the form of the relevant grammatical item and comments on its use. This is not a grammar of abstract rules; it shows that the forms have meanings.

3

THE GRAMMAR TOOLBOX

A TOOLBOX FULL OF WORDS

In Chapter 2 we understood grammar through the metaphor of building blocks, and how we put the pieces together in chains and nests to create structures and a whole system, like a completed building, from ground floor to roof. In this chapter, we see grammar more as a box of tools which can be used to do different jobs and create different types of meanings.

Words are where grammar and vocabulary meet. Words belong to **word classes**. Nouns, verbs, adjectives and adverbs are the major word classes. Determiners, pronouns, prepositions and conjunctions belong in the minor word classes. In this chapter, we will look at the major classes, then in Chapter 4, the minor ones, to see what types of meanings they typically express.

WHAT ARE NOUNS FOR?

NAMING THE WORLD

Nouns give names to people and things. A 'thing' can be a non-human animal, a place, an object, an idea, a feeling, anything we can attach a name to. Table 3.1 shows some examples.

HOW MUCH COFFEE MAKES A COFFEE?

Nouns can show **number**, whether there is one of something (singular – *student*) or more than one (plural – *students*). English has

Table 3.1 Nouns and meanings

Noun	Type of name
student	a person, **common noun** (name of a class of people)
Joanna Smith	a person, **proper noun** (name of an individual)
corner	a place, common noun (name of a class of places)
Washington	a place, proper noun (name of an individual place)
giraffe	a non-human animal
bicycle	a thing, a **concrete** noun
love	an **abstract** noun, an idea or emotion

two different ways of counting things, using different types of nouns. Nouns can either label the world as people and things which can be counted, or as 'stuff', which can't be counted. Consider the nouns in Table 3.2, divided into the two types.

The nouns in the left-hand column name things which can be counted and made plural (*two teabags, a document, three bicycles, a journey, ten green bottles*, etc.). In the right-hand column are things we don't count because English thinks of them as 'stuff'. So we don't use *a(n)* before them (*I bought coffee for my new coffee-maker / I don't eat meat / travel broadens the mind / I hate sitting in traffic / I bought some new furniture*). We call the 'thing' nouns **countable** or **count** nouns; the 'stuff' nouns are **uncountable, non-count** or

Table 3.2 Nouns as things and nouns as stuff

Things	Stuff
teabag	tea
bicycle	traffic
document	information
journey	travel
sausage	meat
bottle	water
tip	advice
chair	furniture
storm	thunder

mass nouns. From now on, we will use countable and uncountable as our standard terms.

Countable nouns in the singular need a **determiner** before them. Determiners are words like *a(n), the, my, your, her, this*. It is not standard English to say *✶Can I borrow pen?* We say *Can I borrow your/the/this/that/a pen?* Chapter 4 has more on determiners.

Uncountable nouns are not used in the plural. We don't say *furnitures, informations, advices*. To talk about specific examples of uncountable nouns we have to say *a piece of furniture, some useful bits of information, a good piece of advice*, and so on. But when I go to a café, I can ask for *two coffees*, and the local supermarket has a counter marked *cold meats*. We can sometimes turn uncountable 'stuff' into countable 'things'. We can order *three teas and a coffee* in a café, we can say *Hamlet is a work by Shakespeare*, but we don't say *I've got a new work* when we mean *I've got a new job*.

This distinction between countable and uncountable affects what words can come before the nouns. We do not normally say *a quantity of children failed the exam because it was too hard* (we say *a number of children*) and we don't say *the number of rice you need for this dish is 100 grams* (we say *the quantity/amount of rice*). But do not be surprised if you hear someone say *the amount of people who shop online has increased*; such things are flexible and always on the move. *Amount* has expanded its territory so that now people use it with countable and uncountable nouns.

INFORMATION ADD-ON

Uncountable nouns can be used with a(n) when we mean 'a type of':
   It's best to use a very strong cheese for this recipe (a very strong type of)
Some nouns are only used in the plural:
   binoculars, glasses (to improve vision), *shorts, trousers, pants, scissors*

Some languages do not have the countable–uncountable distinction in the same way as English does and there are differences among varieties of English. British English generally avoids making the noun *accommodation* plural, but American English allows *student accommodations*, and American English forms are often absorbed into British English. Malaysian English, although it is linked historically to British English, also makes some nouns plural which in British English are uncountable, and linguists have noted plurals such as *staffs* (people employed at a workplace), *accommodations* and *jewelleries* in Malaysian usage (Yamaguchi and Deterding 2016).

CORPUS EVIDENCE

Here are some extracts from recordings of Singaporean English speakers. What might a speaker of standard British or North American English notice about countable and uncountable usage in the Singapore variety?

I don't like horror movie.
That's just a hearsay.
I only have er two or three lecture in school.
    (extracts taken from the *NIE Corpus of Spoken Singapore English*: http://videoweb.nie.edu.sg/phonetic/niecsse/saal-quarterly.htm)

WHAT ELSE CAN NOUNS DO?

Some nouns tell us the sex of a person or animal (*boy, girl, actress, bull*). This is not the same as the **gender** of a noun in languages such as French and Spanish. In Spanish, a car (*un coche*) is 'masculine', a house (*una casa*) is 'feminine'. Gender in different languages is often quite arbitrary and has nothing to do with logic. The word for a car happens to be masculine in Spanish but feminine in French. English does not have that kind of gender difference in nouns.

Suffixes often give us a clue as to which word class a word belongs to. Endings such as *-ion, -ment, -ism, -ness* usually indicate a noun: *extension, excitement, plagiarism, happiness* are all nouns. People often create new meanings by deliberately taking a word from one class and using it as if it belonged to a different class. This is called **class conversion**. When someone says *that's a big ask*, they are using the word *ask* as a noun (we know that because it has the indefinite article 'a' and the adjective *big* in front of it). Most of the time, *ask* will be used as a verb.

CORPUS EVIDENCE

Here are some extracts taken from a corpus. We see some words which are functioning as nouns but which are not normally used as nouns:

[from an advertisement for a travel company] **no ifs, no buts** ... *the price confirmed to you at the time of booking is the price you pay.*
she's had **some ups and downs** *in recent times*
sorry, **my bad**

(all extracts from the Spoken BNC2014)

The expressions *no ifs, no buts* uses conjunctions as if they were nouns. *Up* and *down* are usually prepositions or adverbs, not nouns. *Bad* is an example of a word that most people used only as an adjective but which has recently been used as a noun with *my* to mean the same as *my fault/my mistake*. Word classes are an abstraction based on how words are most typically used. We can only reliably tell what class a word belongs to by seeing it in context. If a dictionary labels a word as a noun, it is only because the lexicographers (dictionary-makers) have observed it most often used that way.

BUILDING WITH NOUNS

As we saw in Chapter 2, noun phrases can express quite complex meanings. The **head** of a noun phrase is the noun around which the rest of the phrase is built. All noun phrases have a head, even if the phrase consists of just one word. Table 3.3 shows some simple and more complex noun phrases.

Notice how the noun phrase can extend in both directions from the head and can include quite a few words.

Things before the head in the noun phrase are **pre-modifiers**; they 'modify' or alter the meaning of the noun. In the table, after the first row, *music* is modified to include only traditional English folk, not modern Irish classical, not heavy metal American rock.

Things after the head are **post-modifiers**. They tell us more about the head, for example restricting it to just one occasion

Table 3.3 Noun phrases

← ————————————————— *Noun phrase* ————————————————— →		
Pre-modifiers	*Head*	*Post-modifiers*
	music	
traditional	music	
traditional folk	music	from the nineteenth century
traditional English folk	music	from the nineteenth century recorded on wax cylinders
the traditional English folk	music	which they played on the radio yesterday

when the music was heard (*which they played on the radio yesterday*) or something else which limits the range of interpretation (*recorded on wax cylinders*, not on tape or vinyl discs).

VERBS: BEING, DOING, HAPPENING

WHO DOES WHAT AND TO WHOM?

Many of us will recall being told at school (if you did grammar at school, that is!) that verbs are 'action' words. This is true of verbs like *run, eat, shout, drive*, but other verbs describe states (*be, have, feel*) or events (*decrease, happen, evolve*). Because of that, it is easier to think of verbs as 'process' words, as we did in Chapter 2. Processes are at the centre of relationships between the participants in a clause.

MAIN VERBS, AUXILIARIES AND MODALS

The verbs that describe actions, states and events like *run, shout, feel* and *happen* are often called **main verbs** or **lexical verbs** ('lexical' because they are part of the lexis or vocabulary of English). But verbs can express other types of meaning too. One type of meaning is expressed by **auxiliary verbs**, the other type by **modal verbs**. These other verbs are short, one-syllable verbs and they are very common in English. They are small verbs with big meanings.

AUXILIARY 'BE': MARKING ASPECT

As well as acting as a main verb in the famous words of Shakespeare's Hamlet, 'To be or not to be', the verb *be* often acts as an auxiliary verb. **Auxiliary verbs** tell us more about how the process expressed by the main verb should be interpreted.

Be has an important part to play in how we talk about events. We can use it to contrast meanings such as *I **work** on Mondays* and *I'm not **working** this week*. The second sentence uses auxiliary *be* plus the *-ing* form (or **present participle**) of a main verb.

I'm not working and *I was not working* describe an ongoing process, one where we are plunged into the middle without focussing on its start or finish. For this reason, we call it **continuous** or **progressive aspect**. From now on, we will use the term continuous. 'Aspect' points to what features of a process the speaker wants to pay attention to. *I work* and *I worked* express a different aspect of the event compared with *I am/was working*, one where the beginning and end points are relevant. This is called **simple aspect**. Table 3.4 compares these two aspects.

Not all languages have this kind of contrast: Spanish does, and marks it in a similar way to English. Swedish does not and has to beat about the bush a little to specify the continuous meaning. As always, logic has nothing to do with it; this is simply a convention of English grammar.

To understand the simple versus continuous concept, imagine you are an astronaut standing on the moon. You look at the

Table 3.4 Simple and continuous aspect

Example	Aspect and comment
It always rains when we go camping.	Simple: The rain is seen as a complete event which happens regularly.
It's raining again!	Continuous: We are in the middle of the rain. When it started and when it will finish are not relevant.
I was looking for my car keys all day yesterday.	Continuous: When I started and finished is not the point. At any and every point in the day I was engaged in the activity.
I looked everywhere for my car keys but couldn't find them.	Simple: The whole event, the search for my keys, was a failure from start to finish.

earth – there are events going on all the time there, but you are not in the middle of them. You are observing them from the outside, and the earth has a line around its edge, a boundary that separates it from outer space. English simple aspect is like that. You are an observer on the outside of events. Now come back down to earth. Wherever you are on the earth, whichever direction you go, you are still in the middle of everything and the globe has no edges where you fall off the planet. As the physicist Stephen Hawking so humorously said: 'Reports of people falling off are thought to be exaggerations' (Hawking 2001: 85). The boundless planet is like continuous aspect; we are always in the midst of it.

AUXILIARY 'HAVE': MARKING ASPECT

Another type of aspect uses the verb *have*. This is **perfect aspect**. Perfect aspect is formed with *have* plus the past participle (sometimes also known as the *-en* form) of the main verb. Consider these examples and how they are different from the continuous/progressive aspect with *be*:

*I've **spoken** to Jim about the broken fence.*
*Born in 1998, she **has lived** in Stockholm all her life.*
*Liz **had left** by the time we got there.*
*I **had wanted** a hat like that for years.*

Perfect aspect is a way of talking about a process in terms of another point in time. With *have* in the present tense (*I've spoken, she **has** lived*), the speaker is saying that something is relevant to the present moment of speaking, perhaps because it is newsworthy, perhaps it has just happened and is still fresh in the speaker's mind, or because it continues to happen up to the present, or simply that it is linked in some unspecified way to the present. We call this the **present perfect**. Table 3.5 shows this visually.

With *had*, the speaker is saying something was relevant to a time in the past (to 'then', not 'now'), so we call it the **past perfect**.

The examples in Table 3.6 are in the simple aspect of the perfect, but we can bring the continuous aspect in too, and combine its meanings with the perfect meanings.

Table 3.5 Present perfect and relevance to 'now'

←——————————————————TIME ——————————————————→	NOW
	I've spoken to Jim about the broken fence.
	Our next-door neighbour has bought a sports car.
Born in 1998, she has lived in Stockholm all her life.————————→	

Table 3.6 Past perfect

←———————————————TIME ———————————————→	THEN
Liz **had left** by the time we got there. We got there (e.g. 3 pm yesterday).	
[e.g. I saw one like that years before] I **had** always **wanted** a hat like that.——————————————————————————————→	

REFLECTION POINT

One winter's morning, my wife looked out of the window and said, 'It's been snowing!'

At the moment she spoke, there was no snow falling. Why did she use the continuous form? Why not just say 'It has snowed!'?

AUXILIARY 'BE': MARKING VOICE

The contrast between active and passive voice also involves auxiliary *be*:

*Duncan **wrote** the report.*
*The report **was written** by Duncan.*

The reality is the same in both cases: Duncan is the 'doer' or agent of the process, and the report is on the receiving end of the

Table 3.7 Perfect aspect: Continuous form

	have	*be*	*-ing form*	
My car	has	been	making	strange noises lately.
George	had	been	standing	in the queue for hours.

process. What has changed is who or what is expressed as the grammatical subject of the verb − in the first case Duncan, in the second case the report.

ASPECT AND VOICE: USING THE TOOLS TOGETHER

We can combine the two aspects (continuous and perfect) with passive voice. Table 3.8 shows this; the verbs are in the **perfect continuous passive**. The pattern is complex and not very common, but it conforms to standard grammar. It is here to illustrate how a complex verb phrase can be built up and the meanings it can express. You may get tongue-twisted if you try saying too many of these quickly!

AUXILIARY 'DO': YES OR NO?

In some languages, if you want to ask a question, you just flip the subject and the verb. In French if you want to ask someone if they like a song, you can say *Aimes-tu cette chanson?*, which is literally, *Like you this song*? This doesn't work for most verbs in English. We can invert the subject and verb with *be* and *have* as main verbs, though doing it with *have* can sound rather formal (V = verb, S = subject):

V   S
Are you *an engineer?*
Have you *any cousins?* (formal)

Table 3.8 Aspects and voice combined

	Have	*Be*	*Be*	*Main verb*	
She	has	been	being	pestered	by salespeople.
He	had	been	being	asked	for ages to stand for president.

English gets around the problem by using auxiliary *do*, which enables the speaker to flip the auxiliary verb and subject while keeping the main verb in its usual position, after the subject:

Aux S   V   O
Do   you *have any cousins?*
Did your friend *get the job?*

Likewise, English negative statements use *do*, where other languages just use a negative word. *Yo no hablo francés* in Spanish means literally *I not speak French; Jag pratar inte franska* in Swedish literally means *I speak not French*, which in English sounds like something a character in a Shakespeare play would say! Here are some examples of English negative statements:

*She **doesn't** own a laptop.*
*I **didn't** understand a word of that lecture.*
*The Prime Minister **does not** agree.*

We can combine both patterns with *do* in negative interrogatives:

Don't you *like garlic?*
Doesn't she *want to come with us?*
Didn't the salesperson *ring you back? They promised they would.*

INFORMATION ADD-ON

In some varieties of English and when speakers want to be a bit more emphatic, or if they already think the answer is no, *not* can be used after the subject:

Aux S   not V   O
Do you not *like garlic?*
Does she not *want to come with us?*
Did the salesperson not *ring you back? They promised they would.*

AUXILIARY 'DO' FOR EMPHASIS

We can use *do* as an emphatic auxiliary in an affirmative (positive) statement when we really want to express something strongly:

*I **do** get annoyed when people sit in their cars with the engine running. Should we call a doctor? She **does** look terribly pale.*

SUBSTITUTE 'DO'

Do can also be used to substitute for information that we don't want to repeat (often with *so* or *that*). Instead of saying (a), we can say (b):

a   *He promised he would support us, and he supported us.*
b   *He promised he would support us, and he **did**/**did so**/**did that**.*

MODAL VERBS: WHAT'S TRUE, WHAT'S RIGHT

Modal verbs in English are verbs such as *can, could, shall, should, will, would, may, might, must, have to* and other, less common ones like *ought (to)* and *need*. There are two main types of meaning that modal verbs express. The first is to do with talking about what is true, certain, probable or possible. The second expresses what the speaker thinks is right, desirable or obligatory. The technical terms for these two types are **epistemic modality** and **deontic modality**, though you may rarely need to use that terminology.

THAT COULD BE TRUE ... TO A DEGREE

Modality is very useful for hedging statements. Hedging means using language in a way that allows you not to commit 100 per cent to something. Consider these examples:

1   *A week from now I **will** be 40.*
2   *It **can** rain quite a lot in Ireland in August.*
3   *All the lights are off. They **must** be out.*
4   *Humans **could** land on Mars within ten years.*
5   *The decorating **should** be finished by about next Wednesday.*
6   *The repairs **might** cost a lot more than we think.*

These modal verbs allow you to position yourself relative to the truth or certainty of what you wish to say. Sentence (1) is

unhedged; the speaker is certain. (2) is also a confident statement: Based on past experience, the speaker knows this does in fact happen. (3) is a confident assertion based on the immediate evidence. (4) is less certain, but there is reason to believe it is a possibility. (5) is a less confident assumption or estimate and (6) is something the speaker is not at all certain about but suspects. Life is rarely a simple picture of true and not true, and modality is at the heart of our experience of life as a series of grey areas. Success in fields such as academic writing or business negotiations can be affected by strategic use of modal verbs. No-one likes to be too certain or dogmatic.

'YOU MUST COME TO DINNER SOMETIME!'

I am often tempted to respond to such an invitation by saying, 'Okay, I'll come this evening,' just to see the expression on the other person's face. But I know the speaker just means 'It would be nice/desirable if you came to dinner one day.' *Must* is a verb which can express deontic meanings, that is meanings connected with what the speaker thinks is right, obligatory, desirable, ideal, etc. We saw in example (3) in the previous section that it can also express an epistemic meaning – this is true of several of the modal verbs.

To say to someone 'You must be here by five o'clock' is quite strong. We can say 'You should be here by five o'clock' or 'You need to be here by five o'clock,' which are less of an imposition on the other person. We call this considering the other person's **face**, and a threat to someone's face or loss of face through being bossed around is not something anyone wants.

REFLECTION POINT

Consider the degree of obligation these sentences impose on the listener and the potential loss of face they might cause. How could they be made less face-threatening?

You can't take that on board the plane.

You have to listen to your parents' advice.

If you're unhappy, you must look for a new job.

Skill and strategy in the use of deontic modality, or lack of it, can determine success or failure in human relations. I always hoped, when I was a full-time academic, that if I said to one of my students, 'You might want to read Ronald Carter's book on vocabulary' they would understand 'Read it or else!'

WE USE SMALL VERBS AS TAG VERBS, DON'T WE ... OR DO WE?

The auxiliary and modal verbs are very useful for tagging on to questions, statements and commands in spoken language. How you use them sends out signals as to how you would like the listener to respond.

The first two types put pressure on the listener to confirm what the speaker is asserting. A challenge on the part of the listener (A: *He doesn't drive, does he?* B: *Oh yes, he does!*) could be face-threatening.

Table 3.9 Tag-types

Clause type	Example	Tag type	Comment
affirmative	You **like** horror films, **don't** you? She **works** in London, **doesn't** she?	negative question tag	I'm pretty sure − please confirm.
negative	We **shouldn't** waste any more time, **should** we? He **doesn't** drive, **does** he?	affirmative question tag	I'm pretty sure − please confirm.
affirmative	She **can** speak Russian, **can** she? I **could** have done it online, **could** I?	affirmative question tag	I don't really know for sure. Please tell me.
affirmative	He **speaks** three languages, he **does**. I'**m** so forgetful, I **am**.	affirmative statement tag	I'm confident that this is so.
imperative	**Turn** that music down, **will** you! **Carry** this for me, **would** you? **Let's** go home, **shall** we?	imperative tag	Reinforces a command, request or suggestion.

MIGHT I ASK YOU A QUESTION?

Another way in which English uses modal verbs is for making requests. There is quite a difference between the first of the following sentences and the last two.

Pass me that chair.
Will you pass me that chair.
Can you pass me that chair.
Would you pass me that chair.
Could you pass me that chair.

The modal verbs enable us to soften requests, instructions, commands, etc. The same applies to asking permission:

Can I ask a question?
Could I ask a question? (a little less direct)
May I ask a question? (slightly more formal)
Might I ask a question? (rather formal)

The modal verbs are part of the system of politeness in English; choices we make in using them can either protect and respect the other person's face or threaten it and potentially damage relations. It all depends on context and the relationship which exists between the speaker and the listener.

HOW LONG IS A PIECE OF STRING?

As before (see Table 3.8, above), it is possible to create quite long strings of verbs starting with a modal verb. We can combine modal verbs with auxiliary verbs that express aspect and voice. A string of five verbs, as in the final example, is rare.

*We **should have thought** of that.* (modal + perfect)
*They **will be arriving** next week.* (modal + continuous)
*She **must have been waiting** all day!* (modal + perfect + continuous)
*That yogurt **should have been** eaten by the 23rd.* (modal + perfect + passive)
*He **could have been being interviewed** for a job or something.* (modal + perfect + continuous + passive)

These are little verbs with big meanings. Grammar is not just about rules and correctness. It is about how we interact with one another.

COLOURING IN THE WORLD: ADJECTIVES AND ADVERBS

WHAT'S IT LIKE AND HOW DID IT GO?

We can describe a person or thing in various ways, and we can also describe processes in various ways. These two types of description correspond to the major jobs that **adjectives** and **adverbs** do in the language. Adjectives are words which describe the nature, qualities, characteristics, etc. of people and things. Adverbs can be used to describe the circumstances surrounding a process, often telling us where, how or when a process takes place. We will see that adverbs can do other things too.

ADJECTIVES: TELLING IT LIKE IT IS

In speaking, we usually find just one or two adjectives before a noun. In writing, especially formal, academic and creative writing, we may find more. In the Spoken BNC2014 corpus, for example, we find only a couple of occasions when two adjectives are used before the word *bridge* (*old wooden bridge, tiny little bridge*). In the written BNC corpus, we find longer strings of adjectives, including this one: *the characteristic rural Swiss timber-built covered bridge* (BNC1994 FTU), which has five adjectives before *bridge*, and which would be quite a mouthful to say quickly in ordinary conversation! When there are several adjectives strung together, how do we choose which order to put them in?

REFLECTION POINT

Consider these different versions of the same noun phrases. In each case, the version in bold is the original from the British national Corpus (BNC1994). Consider why that order seems most likely.

1(a) non mass-produced olive Italian extra virgin oil
1(b) extra virgin non mass-produced olive Italian oil

1(c) **non mass-produced Italian extra virgin olive oil** (BNC1994 FBL)

2(a) **splendid bronze cauldrons** (BNC1994 J250)

2(b) bronze splendid cauldrons

3(a) a healthy nice red rosy colour

3(b) **a nice healthy rosy red colour** (BNC1994 J1H)

3(c) a rosy nice healthy red colour

It is apparent that some orders are better or more natural-sounding than others, even though others are possible. What seems to be a general rule of thumb is that the adjectives go from the more subjective (*splendid, nice, healthy*) towards more objective features (*Italian, bronze, red*) before we get to the noun. And if one of the words describing the noun is itself a noun, that tends to be near the head noun (e.g. *bronze, olive*).

These are not hard and fast rules and different emphases can be created by shifting the words around. For example, another BNC corpus example mentions *an extremely rare short-nosed white bellied dolphin* (BNC1994 J2T). The possible alternative *a short-nosed white bellied extremely rare dolphin* would be saying things in a slightly different way. Word order can be changed for effect; poets do this frequently. But some word orders just sound very odd indeed, so a basic, general convention is at work, even though it may not always be obvious.

Traditionally, when we use more than one adjective before a noun, commas should separate all but the last one, so we may prefer to write *rural, Swiss, timber-built, covered bridge*, but be prepared to see this 'rule' observed in the breaking of it.

ADVERBS: HOW DID IT GO?

We tend to answer questions like this with reactions such as *It went really well / badly. Well* and *badly* are **adverbs**. Adverbs mostly end in *-ly* (*quickly, sadly, hopefully, carefully*), though some everyday ones don't (sing *well*, drive *fast*, work *hard*, finish *now*, come *here*). They can tell us about when something happens (*now, then, tomorrow* – **time adverbs**), where it happens (*here, there, everywhere, down-stairs* – **place adverbs**), how we do something (*well, carefully,* *stupidly, politely* – **manner adverbs**), or how often something happens (*often, never, regularly* – **frequency adverbs**).

Adverbs are very versatile words. They can attach themselves to adjectives or to other adverbs. In the first sentence in this paragraph, *very* is an adverb attached to the adjective *versatile*. *Very* modifies the adjective by telling us to what extent or degree what the adjective says is true. *Very* is a **degree adverb**. Other examples of degree adverbs are *extremely* well, *almost* ready, *too* fast, *highly* educated.

ADVERBS AS ADVERBIALS

Something can go *well* or *badly*. We can drive *slowly* or *carefully*. Table 3.10 shows examples of different adverbs acting as adverbials.

In Table 3.10, we see the following:

- *Too fast*: Degree adverb + adverb of manner
- *Yesterday*: Adverb of time
- *Always*: Adverb of frequency
- *Very carefully:* Degree adverb + adverb of manner

In English, bringing things to the front of the clause focuses on or emphasises them. We might want to create a contrast (**Normally** she drives slowly, but **yesterday** she drove too fast), or simply to make a point stronger (**Stupidly**, I forgot to charge my phone, and ran out of battery).

Table 3.10 Adverbs acting as adverbials

1	She		drove	**too fast**.	
2	She		drove	to Edinburgh	**yesterday**.
4	She	**Always**	drives	**very carefully**.	

REFLECTION POINT

Try inserting the adverbs in capitals into different places in the sentences, including at the front. What effect does it have? Do some positions sound less natural?

1   I had never considered doing a PhD. PREVIOUSLY
2   Everyone had finished the task. SOON
3   You will see a small bakery. NEARBY
4   She left the room. SUDDENLY

You might have noticed that not all possible places work equally well in sentences 1–4. *Soon* sounds most natural at the front of number 2 or after *had*. *Previously* is quite flexible. *Nearby* fits nicely at the front, or at the end and after *see*. However, 2 and 4 sound odd if we put the adverb immediately after the main verb (*finished soon the task, left suddenly the room*). Generally speaking, and unlike some other languages, English does not like adverbs to intrude on the space between a verb and its direct object.

CONCLUSION

In this chapter we have seen how the major word classes of noun, verb, adjective and adverb create different types of meanings and do different types of work in the clause as subjects, verbs, objects, complements and adverbials. Later in the book we will return to some of the apparently dry and innocuous features of grammar and see just how controversial they can be.

FURTHER READING

Seely, J. 2013. *Oxford A–Z of Grammar and Punctuation*. Oxford: Oxford University Press.
Because of its A–Z format, you can readily access the entries on each of the major word classes, where you will find further information on the subjects covered in this chapter. The book includes a number of charts and diagrams which make the word classes easier to understand.

McCarthy, M. J. 2021. *Innovations and Challenges in Grammar*. London: Routledge.
In chapter 3, I trace the development of grammars in the eighteenth and nineteenth century, where we see changes in the way the English grammatical system was conceived and presented. Slowly but surely, we see less of an emphasis on

words and word classes and a move towards looking at how everything works together in clauses and sentences.

Biber, D., Johansson, S., Leech, G., Conrad, S. and Finegan, E. 1999. *Longman Grammar of Spoken and Written English.* **London: Longman.**
Section C of this reference grammar (pages 229–566) covers all the word classes in a detailed way, but you can dip in and out of it to read about specific topics (e.g. nouns, adverbs). As with the rest of the book, the authors give examples of how the word classes are differently distributed across different types of text, for example, how conversation has fewer nouns than fiction, news texts or academic writing. This is done through reader-friendly charts based on corpus evidence.

4

THE GRAMMAR TOOLBOX CONTINUED

THE OTHER WORD CLASSES

SMALL WORDS GET EVERYWHERE

If you do a frequency count of a corpus of present-day British English, you will find that most of the very common words are grammar items; they are not lexical words like *bumblebee, cauterise, persistently* or *makeshift*, but words like *the, my, some, to, here, on, and, what, this, but*. Most of these everyday words are short, one-syllable words, but they have important jobs to do in creating meaning.

CORPUS EVIDENCE

These lists show the top 20 most frequent words in the written section of the British National Corpus (BNC1994) and the Spoken BNC2014 corpus.

Table 4.1 Top 20 most frequent words (BNC)

	Written	Spoken
1	the	I
2	be	be
3	of	it
4	to	you
5	and	the
6	a	and

	Written	*Spoken*
7	in	yeah
8	that	that
9	is	a
10	for	to
11	it	n't
12	was	like
13	on	do
14	with	of
15	as	was
16	be	they
17	he	in
18	I	so
19	by	but
20	at	is
21	are	he

Number 11, *n't*, doesn't look like a 'word', but the corpus engineers have told the computer to count it as a short form of the negative *not*, which is a grammar word. In Chapter 6 and Chapter 8 we will see that *like* (number 12 in the spoken list) is not all that it appears to be and is not an intruder. It is not the 'like' of loving and fondness.

The most common words are members of **closed systems**. Closed systems are groups of words related to one another to which we don't normally add new members. An example of a closed system in English is the set *this, that, these, those*. It has four members, and we cannot easily invent a fifth. *This* and *these* mean 'near' (physically or mentally), *that* and *those* mean 'distant' (physically or mentally). We call this the demonstrative system; the four words are **demonstratives**. Spanish has a different demonstrative system, with three different sets of words roughly meaning 'near me', 'near you' and 'not near either of us' with respect to the speaker and the listener. Whenever we look at languages around the world, we see that the way they divide up the 'mental space' is reflected in their grammar and vocabulary. No language is superior or more logical than any other; they are just different.

Other examples of closed systems in English are pronouns (*I, you, she*, etc.), articles (*a(n)/the/no article*), the modal verbs (*can, may, must*, etc., see Chapter 3) and prepositions (*to, of, at, in*, etc.). In this chapter we will look at the main 'smaller words', the sort of work they do and the sorts of meanings they can express.

PRONOUNS

GETTING PERSONAL

The frequency lists above contain the words *I, you, it, they* and *he*. These are **pronouns**, because they can 'stand in for' the people and things which nouns refer to (*pro-nouns*). They can be divided into **personal** and **indefinite** pronouns, and according to whether they are first, second or third person, singular or plural, male or female, whether they can operate as subjects or objects, or both, or whether they can show possession (**possessive pronouns**). Table 4.2 shows a traditional picture of the personal pronouns.

You may be thinking: What about *my, your, our* and *their*? They are used before nouns (*my house, his car, their children*, etc.) and we will look at them separately in the section on **determiners** below. *Myself, yourself* etc. are in the section on **reflexive pronouns** below. You may also be wondering: Why should *he, him* and *his* come before *she, her* and *hers*? Recall I said this is 'a traditional picture'. In Chapter 8 we will see how this has changed.

A pronoun which is not in Table 4.2 is *one*, as in *One must always do one's duty*. *One* is special in that it does not specify any particular person and can mean 'any person at all', 'me, you and

Table 4.2 Personal pronouns

Person	Singular	Plural	Subject	Object	Possessive
First	I	we	I/we	me/us	mine/ours
Second	you	you	you	you	yours
Third	he/she/it	they	he/she/it/they	him/her/it/them	his/hers/theirs

everyone who thinks like us', or sometimes 'me and people like me but not you' – in fact it is often quite vague in who it refers to. It is a **generic** pronoun. It is also considered rather formal and posh. In more informal language, most people use *you* for the meanings covered by *one*, for example, *You can't trust anyone nowadays, can you? / You have to pay more if you want the full version of the program.* This is called **generic *you***.

One(s) can also be used as a substitute pronoun, as in *Which shoes do you want, the black **ones** or the brown **ones**?*

We can also use *we* (as I have just done) to refer to everyone, and we can use it to refer to different groups of people, but it may have different interpretations. For instance, *We're away next week. Have you forgotten?* is, on the face of it, ambiguous: It could mean 'you and I will be away', or it could mean 'somebody else and I will be away but not you'. Some languages have separate words for these 'inclusive' and 'exclusive' uses of *we* (e.g. Bahasa Malaysia); in English *we* depends on the context for its meaning.

In informal contexts, the pronoun *they* can have the meaning of 'authorities' (e.g. the government, the local authority), for example *They're building a new bridge on the M24.* We do not need to specify who *they* are. In more formal contexts, we might want to use the passive voice and say *A new bridge is being built on the M24.*

ME AND MY SISTER: SUBJECT AND OBJECT PRONOUNS

In more formal contexts, subject pronouns are used when the person referred to is part of the subject of the verb. In these examples, the subjects are underlined:

<u>My team members and **I**</u> will be happy to discuss this with you.
<u>**I** and my team members</u> will be happy to discuss this with you.
<u>**She** and her brother</u> were both born in New Zealand.

In informal situations, especially in everyday conversation, people often use object pronouns even when the person referred to is part of the subject, especially when the pronoun comes first:

<u>**Me** and my brother</u> used to go hiking in Scotland.
<u>My father and **her**</u> never got along together.

On the other hand, we often find people using subject pronoun *I* instead of *me* to sound more polite and less egotistic (less of 'me-me-me') after a preposition when two participants are involved. Prepositions traditionally take object pronouns:

*If you have any questions, do not hesitate to contact **Simon or I**, and we can talk things over.* (email from a financial adviser)
*Please keep this news **between you and I** until it is made official.*

In the first example, if Simon was not included, the email writer would almost certainly have said:

*If you have any questions, do not hesitate to contact **me**, and we can talk things over.*

Appropriate choices depend on the context and the type of relationship that exists between speakers and listeners.

REFLEXIVE PRONOUNS: GRAMMATICAL SELFIES

The pronouns *myself, yourself, itself, himself, herself, oneself, ourselves* and *themselves* are **reflexive pronouns**. They are used in two main ways: To indicate that two participants in the clause (e.g. subject and object) are the same person or thing, and to emphasise a noun or pronoun.

*She promised **herself** a holiday when all the work was over.* (subject and object are the same person)
*The President **herself** was not present at the gathering.* (emphatic)
***Myself** I would never have said such a foolish thing.* (emphatic)

There is also a 'polite' use of the reflexive pronouns when people feel an ordinary personal pronoun might be too blunt or direct.

*Martin and **myself** would like discuss this with you at some point.* (or *Martin and I*)
*We'll leave it with **yourselves** to make the final decision.* (or *with you*)

This very morning, I received an email from a firm of accountants which ended: *If you require anything from ourselves, please feel free to get in touch.* The email writer clearly felt that to say *anything from us* was less appropriate to the situation.

EACH OTHER AND ONE ANOTHER

Each other and *one another* are **reciprocal pronouns**, used when an action or state applies equally between two or more people or things. Normally, *each other* is used when there are two people or things involved; *one another* is for more than two.

*Ken and Jane dislike **each other** intensely.* (Ken dislikes Jane and Jane dislikes Ken)
*The committee members are always disagreeing with **one another**.* (several individuals disagreeing with other individuals)

However, this is a rule that is only loosely applied, and the two forms are often used interchangeably. In this example of *one another*, just two cities are involved:

*I know for sure that Pompeii and Rome are a long way away from **one another*** (Spoken BNC2014 SASC)

IS ANYONE OUT THERE?

Not all pronouns refer to specific people or things. The pronoun *it* can refer to an animal, either as an individual or as a member of a class:

*That cat's unusual; **it** has one black ear and one white.*
*A cat always knows where **it** lives.*

In these examples, *it* is used instead of repeating *that cat* or *a cat*. We can also use *it* to refer to something present in the context or elsewhere in the text:

*Look at all those people fighting to get into the shop. **It**'s just crazy!* (the immediate situation)
***It** always amazes me that most people can't read maps.* (it stands for what follows after the verb, sometimes called the 'dummy it'; more formally we could say *That most people cannot read maps always amazes me*)

WHAT IT'S ALL ABOUT: CLEFTS

Compare these examples:

The tree got damaged, not the wall.
It was the tree that got damaged, not the wall.
You need to see Elizabeth.
It's Elizabeth you need to see.
They arrived late on Thursday.
It was late on Thursday that they arrived.

The versions starting with *it* are *it*-clefts (see Chapter 2). They are used to single out one clause-element, e.g. subject, object or adverbial, to focus on. This can be for contrast (in the first example, *the tree* is contrasted with *the wall*) or to emphasise something important, for example the time something happened in a story (*it was late on Thursday*).

SOMEONE OR OTHER DID IT

Some pronouns are **indefinite** in meaning. These are words like *someone/somebody, something, everything, nothing, none, anyone/anybody, no-one/nobody, somewhere, nowhere.*

REFLECTION POINT

Look at these pairs of sentences. Do you think the choice of pronoun makes any difference? If so, what?

Someone was trying to contact you this morning.
Somebody was trying to contact you this morning.
Does anybody use a camera anymore? Everybody seems to use their phone nowadays.
Does anyone use a camera anymore? Everyone seems to use their phone nowadays.
No-one likes to think they are useless.
Nobody likes to think they are useless.

The Reflection point is asking you to think about the *-one* ending and the *-body* ending for pronouns that begin with *some-, any-, every-* and *no-*. You might have concluded that there isn't really much difference, and, in most cases, it doesn't matter which ending you use. However, in the written texts of the BNC1994, we see a definite preference for the *-one* forms over the *-body* forms. So, if you are concerned with formal academic or formal business writing, for example, you might choose the *-one* forms. If you do not want to sound too formal, you might choose the *-body* forms.

THE ONES WHICH MATTER: RELATIVE PRONOUNS

Relative pronouns are used to introduce relative clauses (see Chapter 2). The most common relative pronouns are *who, whose, whom, which* and *that*.

WHO, WHICH, THAT AND WHOM

Who is used to refer to people; *which* refers to things. *That* can refer to both people and things. The relative clauses are underlined.

1   *The student **who/that** got the highest marks also received a one-hundred-dollar book token.*
2   *The film **which/that** we all enjoyed most was Skyfall.*

Which and *that* can be omitted in (2), because the film is the object of *enjoyed*. They can't be left out when they refer to the subject, e.g. *the student* in (1).

In more formal contexts, *whom* is used when the pronoun refers to the object:

*The politician **whom** everyone admired most was a junior minister in the health department.* (formal; less formal, *who, that* or nothing)

CORPUS EVIDENCE

In Chapter 2 on p. 22, we compared the frequency of *whom* in writing and speaking. We can also observe change over time by subdividing the corpus according to when the data were collected. In barely 20 years from 1974 to 1993, the use of *whom* in the written BNC1994 declined noticeably. *Whom* in the Spoken BNC2014 is extremely rare.

Some dialects use *what* instead of *who, which* or *that,* but it is considered non-standard.

The man **what** *delivered that parcel was from Bulgaria.* (standard: *who* or *that*)
I think that new car **what** *they've bought is ugly.* (standard: *which, that* or nothing)

WHOSE

Whose refers to possession and can be used of persons or things.

The student **whose** *phone rang during the lecture got publicly shamed.*
Cardiff is a city **whose** *position makes it the ideal first stop on a tour of Wales.*

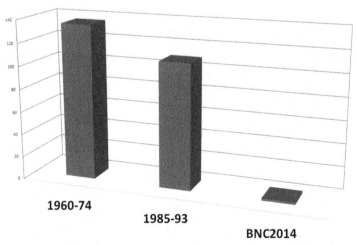

Change in the use of *whom*

1960-74

1985-93

BNC2014

Figure 4.1 Change in the use of *whom* (figures based on per million words).

Or, rather more formally:

*Cardiff is a city the position **of which** makes it the ideal first stop on a tour of Wales.*

WHICH *IN SENTENTIAL RELATIVE CLAUSES (COMMENT CLAUSES)*

Which can be used to introduce a clause that comments on a whole sentence or utterance.

*The repair to the door cost €800, **which** is outrageously expensive.*

In conversation, a *which* comment clause can be added by a different speaker. This is an indication of the way spoken grammar is often jointly constructed.

A   *Every child got the chance to perform.*
B   ***Which** was lovely.*
A   *Yes.*

When this happens, speakers usually do not get indignant and tell their listeners off for intruding into their 'sentences' by adding extra clauses.

INTERROGATIVE PRONOUNS: WHAT ARE THEY FOR?

Interrogative pronouns are used to ask questions where the answer is expected to fill in the 'missing information' which the pronoun is looking for. The interrogative pronouns are *who, whom, whose, which* and *what*.

Although *which* and *what* refer to different types of choice (Table 4.3), *what* is sometimes used in informal situations when there is a simple choice between two alternatives.

What would you rather, pizza or pasta? (choice between two alternatives)

DEMONSTRATIVE PRONOUNS: THIS IS IMPORTANT, THAT'S NOT

This, that, these and *those* are used as pronouns to refer to things either physically or mentally near (*this, these*) or physically or mentally distant (*that, those*).

Table 4.3 Interrogative pronouns

Pronoun	Example	Comment
who	Who ate that pie?	Question about a person as subject
whom	With whom did you work?	Object pronoun after a preposition (*with*). Rather formal. Most people would just say *Who did you work with*?
whose	That's my cap, so whose is this?	Question about possession
which	Which do you want, the black one, the green one or the blue one?	Question about choice from a limited range of options
what	What do you want for dinner?	Question about an open-ended set of choices

[speaker A is holding a cardboard box]

A   *What shall I do with **this**?*

B   *I'll take **that** .*

These *are the photos of my grandparents that I was telling you about.*
Those *are nice shoes. Where did you buy them?*

The 'mental' aspect of the pronouns is important. Speakers and writers can use *this* and *that* to associate themselves with something or distance themselves from something. *This* is often used to focus on important points which a writer wants to bring attention to or to develop in some way. It is like a light shining on the information. For example:

The National Farmers' Union's South East region environmental study group is arguing for a fertiliser cut of about 20 per cent, to be applied across Europe by means of individual farm quotas. **This** should lead to an initial reduction of some 11 per cent in crop production, and the group hope that in the long run, cuts of up to 20 per cent could be achieved. **This** would effectively end the problems of over-production which have interfered with the workings of the European Community's Common Agricultural Policy.

(BNC1994 J2T)

The use of *that* can have the opposite effect, distancing the writer (and possibly the reader) from an idea or a point:

> Sometimes, Andrew's hurt brought on by Ken was deep indeed. 'I remember being in a mood once when he told me, "You'll go mad some day". **That** was very brutal and hurtful when I felt down. But **that** was a small side of the personal relationship. Most of it was helpful and extremely kind.'

(BNC1994 JOW)

In both the previous examples, the writer could have used the pronoun *it* instead of *this* or *that*. *It* provides a more neutral continuity between ideas. These grammatical choices are significant; they can be quite strategic, giving us the option of bringing some things into the foreground and pushing others into the background (McCarthy 1994).

REFLECTION POINT

Consider this corpus extract and try substituting *this* or *that* instead of the pronoun *it* (in bold) at the beginning of the second sentence. What would the effect be?

> Scheduled for completion in 2006, the development will comprise 23 power stations, involving construction of 215 dams and dykes, the flooding of 26,000 sq km of mainly forest land, and the diversion of 19 rivers. **It** could have far reaching effects on the ecology of James Bay, an important wildlife refuge, with increased salinity posing a threat to fish, migratory birds, ringed seals and beluga whales.

(BNC1994 J2W)

DETERMINERS

Determiners are small words which come before nouns. They tell us specific things about the nouns, for example, who the noun belongs to or is related to (*my first car, your cousin, her job*), the number or quantity of something (**twenty** *people*, **some** *wholemeal flour*), where something is in relation to the speaker (**this** *chair*, **those** *old chairs*), whether something is a specific example of something (*it's in **the** fridge*) or an indefinite example of something (*we need **a** new fridge*). Determiners come before any adjectives in noun phrases.

We saw in Chapter 3 that a singular countable noun always needs a determiner before it. We don't say *I've got new computer*. We say *I've got a/my/this new computer*, using a determiner.

ARTICLES: WHERE'S THE CAT?

Table 4.4 shows three sets of sentences. Those on the left contain *a* or *an*, the middle ones contain *the* and the right-hand ones contain neither *a(n)* nor *the*; we call this the **zero article**.

The three columns show the article system. A singular countable noun such as *cat* needs a determiner: *a cat*. A cat is any individual example of an animal that belongs to the class of cats. A TV is any individual example of all the TV sets on the market. *A(n)* is the **indefinite article**; it does not specify which cat, which TV, which child.

The is different. It refers to something definite and specific, so it is called the **definite article**. Definite and specific in this case means 'a specific example of something, which the speaker and listener can be expected to share an understanding of'. In your own home, if a member of your household says *Where's the cat?* you will probably assume it to mean 'our cat, the cat who lives with us', rather than some strange cat from down the road. Similarly, in Table 4.4, *the TV*

Table 4.4 Articles

A(n)	*The*	*Zero article*
Have they got **a** cat?	Where's **the** cat?	
I bought **a** new TV.	Shall I switch **the** TV off?	What's on TV tonight?
A child was standing near the door.	**The** children always come with us when we go to their aunt's.	Children love hide-and-seek games.

means 'the TV set in this house/room that we both know about'. *The children* means 'our children, not someone else's'.

The moon is something we share as occupants of this planet, just like *the stars* (and *the sun, the sky, the universe*). Students and academics who refer to *the university* normally mean 'this/our university, the one where we are'. The same applies to *the country, the government, the President, the Prime Minister*. Unless we specify that we are talking about another, different country, the assumption is that it is the government/President/Prime Minister we share, in the country where we live or find ourselves. This is **shared knowledge**, and it is the most basic function of the definite article – to refer to the knowledge shared between speakers and listeners, readers and writers.

The zero article is used when we want to refer to a whole class of things or to ideas and concepts. In Table 4.4, *TV* with no article sees television as an abstract idea – the broadcasting system that delivers pictures into our homes; *children* refers to all and any children. In Chapter 3, we saw how uncountable nouns are regarded as 'stuff' in English; that is why we don't use *a(n)* with them. We say *furniture, rice, information*, not ⋆*a furniture*, etc., though we can make them definite (*the furniture I bought last year, the rice in this packet, the information I received*). In sentences such as *Life is unpredictable / Art is important in society / Love makes the world go round*, the zero article indicates that life, art and love are being treated as general ideas.

The article system enables us to refer to people and things in different ways, as individuals, as groups or classes, as 'stuff' or general ideas. Some languages do not have articles in the way English does, and even languages which do have definite and indefinite articles often use them in ways different from English.

REFLECTION POINT

Look at this account of a domestic crisis. Do you think the gaps in the text should be filled with *a*, *the* or the zero article? What do your choices confirm about the use of the articles?

A woman (A) comes into the garden and addresses her husband (B):

A   Have you seen _____ cat? I'm worried that she's gone missing.
    She's not in _____ house and I haven't seen her all day. I put
    _____ food out for her in _____ kitchen but she hasn't eaten it.
B   No. she's not in _____ garden. I'll go and look in _____ street.
(B goes out into _____ street. He stops _____ passer-by.)
B   Excuse me, have you seen _____ black cat by any chance?

INTERROGATIVE DETERMINERS

Which and *what* can be used before nouns to ask questions. *Which* refers to a choice or choices from a limited set of options.

Which glass is yours?
Which books do you want to keep from this pile?

   What refers to more open-ended choices or a range of possible answers.

What books have you read lately?

   Whose refers to possession:

Whose gloves are these?

POSSESSIVE DETERMINERS

The possessive determiners are *my, your, his, her, its, our* and *their*, and the possessive -'s (the **apostrophe**; see below). In most respects this system is straightforward, but there is one historical hangover that has caused a shift in the system.

   In the past, many people, especially in formal writing, used *his* with a noun to refer to everyone, not just males. So, sentences such as *A prospective student must submit his application by 31 March* did not mean women need not worry about the deadline. As society changed, and moved towards more equal treatment of the sexes, people became unhappy with this use of the male possessive determiner to refer to men and women. Some preferred to say *his/her application*; others preferred *their application*, putting the plural determiner into service to mean 'male or female'. Both are perfectly acceptable. We shall see in Chapter 8 that the story doesn't end there, and further social change may realign the possessive determiners further.

One common confusion is to mix up *its* and *it's*. *Its* is the possessive determiner; *it's* means *it is*.

*The name of the village owes **its** origin to Viking invaders.*
***It's** a nice day. Let's go for a walk.*

It is likely that the source of this confusion is that an apostrophe often indicates possession, as in *Mary's house* or *the cat's tail*, so people think *it's* is the possessive form, rather than *its*.

POSSESSIVE -'S

The possessive –'s (apostrophe) shows that someone or something belongs to or has a close association with someone or something. Examples:

Jack's phone got stolen.
Amir's brother was at the restaurant.
One should always be able to depend on one's friends.
Australia's foreign policy was focused on East Asia.
The painting's owner is an anonymous billionaire.
My car's wing mirror was vandalized.

A plural noun is written with the apostrophe after the plural *-s* ending. Examples:

*I need the list of member**s'** names.* (all the members)
*All the girl**s'** parents came to meet the new headteacher.* (more than one girl)
*The car**s'** wing mirrors were all vandalised.* (several cars)

Some nouns have irregular plurals, in which case 's is used (*the children**'s** play area, the men**'s** changing rooms, a women**'s** football team*).

Some people's names end in *-s*, like *James* or *Jones* or *Mavis*. The normal practice with these is to add 's *James's car, Mavis's house*.

Some long names such as *Archimedes* and *Aristophanes* normally just add an apostrophe after the final *-s* rather than writing (or even worse, saying!) the cumbersome *Archimedes's* or *Aristophanes's*.

Aristophanes' plays have survived for over two thousand years.
Archimedes' principle is all about buoyancy in fluids.

When two people or things possess or are closely related to the same person or thing, normally just one apostrophe is sufficient:

We're invited to dinner at Rob and Claire's house.

INFORMATION ADD-ON

In some cases of belonging and possession English does not use -'s and prefers a compound noun.

*The **door handle** was jammed.*
*The **piano keys** have become tarnished over the years.*

Sometimes a distinction is made between a general statement of possession (no -'s) and an individual example (-'s).

***Violin** strings can be very expensive.*
*The **violin's** bridge was missing.*

Possessive -'s has been a source of public controversy in the UK, as we shall see in Chapter 8.

CONJUNCTIONS: GETTING IT TOGETHER

COORDINATING

Conjunctions are items which join and link words, phrases and clauses. They 'conjoin' things. The most common type are the coordinating conjunctions *and, but* and *or*, which we looked at in Chapter 3.

Coordinating conjunctions join two items of the same grammatical form (e.g. two nouns, two phrases, two main clauses):

a   *He plays the guitar. He's in a band.*
b   **He plays the guitar and in a band.*
c   *He plays the guitar and he's in a band.*

Sentence (b) is grammatically odd since it combines a noun phrase (*the guitar*) with a prepositional phrase (*in a band*); the link is not between two grammatically equal items. Sentence (c) links two main clauses.

SUBORDINATING

Subordinating conjunctions link main clauses to subordinate clauses and show the relationship between the main and subordinate clause. In Table 4.5, the subordinate clauses are underlined.

Corpus evidence shows that, in informal speaking, the short form *cos* is almost twice as common as the full form *because*. *Cos* would be considered inappropriate in most formal contexts such as business letters or personal profiles in applications, formal speeches, etc.

CORRELATIVE

Correlative conjunctions consist of two parts, each one followed by one of the two items to be joined ('correlated') in a relationship.

Table 4.5 Examples of subordinating conjunctions

Conjunction	Example	Meaning
if	If we have time, we'll pop in and see you.	Relationship of condition
because	She didn't come because she wasn't feeling well.	Relationship of reason or cause
before	Think before you act.	Relationship of time
whenever	Whenever the weather's fine enough, we have breakfast in the garden.	Relationship of time
whereas	My wife likes cycling, whereas I prefer walking.	Relationship of contrast

Table 4.6 Examples of correlative conjunctions

Conjunction	Example	Meaning
either ... or	You can have either chips or boiled potatoes, but not both.	links two choices
neither ... nor	She neither knew what had happened nor did she care.	links two negative ideas
both ... and	Both Nigel and Karen are working at the university now.	links two people or things sharing the same properties
not only ... but also	Not only did they cancel the concert, but they also refused to pay the band.	links two important or notable ideas
whether ... or	He'll have to get a job, whether he wants to or not.	links two alternative conditions

PREPOSITIONS

WHAT ARE THEY FOR?

Prepositions are words used before noun phrases and pronouns to relate them to another word or phrase. They can express a wide range of meanings. In the examples, prepositions are in bold.

*Put that sofa **in** the living room **near** the window.*
*They sell them **at** the shop **on** the corner **of** Green Street.*
*Shall we go there **in** the summer or **at** the New Year?*
*Leave the money **with** me – don't give it **to** her.*

CORPUS EVIDENCE

The 25 most common prepositions in the BNC1994 are *of, in, to, for, on, with, at, by, to, from, in, about, after, like, over, between, through, before, under, against, since, within, without, during, until.*

Prepositions can also be followed by the *-ing* form of a verb acting as a noun, traditionally called the **gerund**.

*Those shoes are **for** cyc**ling**, not **for** run**ning**.*
*I'm looking forward **to** mee**ting** my new colleagues.*

Some prepositional expressions consist of several words, for example, *in front of, out of, next to, apart from, except for*. American English also has *in back of*. In some dialects, the preposition *off of* is used. This is more common in American English than British English:

*Be careful when you step **off** the escalator.*
*They live on a quiet street **off of** the main road.*

PREPOSITIONS: SHOULD WE LEAVE THEM STRANDED?

One traditional rule about prepositions is that they should not end a sentence. This was based on Latin grammar, but the rule should not apply to English just because Latin did not like sentence-final prepositions. These sentences are perfectly acceptable in standard English:

*Have you got something I can cut this string **with**?*
*Who shall I send this **to**?*
*It's too high – I need something to stand **on**.*

The prepositions in bold are sometimes called *stranded* prepositions since they appear to be just hanging at the end of the sentence and not attached to anything. In informal situations, the same sentences with the prepositions attached to their complements sound very stiff and unnatural:

*Have you got something **with which** I can cut this string?*
***To who(m)** shall I send this?*
*It's too high – I need something **on which** to stand.*

In more formal situations, such sentences are more common:

*This is a proposal **with which** everyone can agree.*
*The site **on which** the building stands was once a Roman theatre.*

REFLECTION POINT

The eighteenth-century grammarian Robert Lowth thought that pre-positions used immediately before words like *who* and *which* were more appropriate to what he called 'the solemn and elevated style' (Lowth 1762/1799: 96). As regards stranded prepositions, he accepted that they were used in conversation and that their use 'is an idiom, which our language is strongly inclined to' (95). What is noticeable about this last quote?

NO, NAY, NEVER …

A well-known Irish folk song, The *Wild Rover*, has the chorus:

> And it's no, nay, never,
> No nay never no more
> Will I play the wild rover,
> No never, no more.

The chorus contains a number of words which are used in **negation**, saying that something is not so. Standard English prefers not to 'double up' negative words in the way some other languages do, so that the sentence *I don't never go there no more* is considered overloaded with negatives. Standard English would require *I don't ever go there anymore*, using just one negative word (*n't/not*). How-ever, many dialects of English use double negatives. The dialect examples here have standard versions on the right.

I haven't said nothing to her.	I haven't said anything to her. / I've said nothing to her.
She didn't see no-one.	She didn't see anyone. / She saw no-one.
We don't want none of them.	We don't want any of them. / We want none of them.
I didn't take no chances.	I didn't take any chances. / I took no chances.

The standard versions with affirmative verbs and *nothing, no-one, none* and *no* on the right are more formal than the versions with *not … anything / anyone / any*.

Dialects of English, and languages which double up negative words (for example, Spanish says **no** *quiero* **nada** – 'I don't want nothing'), are no less logical than standard English. Mathematical logic of the kind 'two negatives make a positive' has nothing to do with it.

WHAT ABOUT ALL THOSE OTHER SMALL WORDS?

In speaking, there are lots of things that don't seem to fit easily into the word classes described so far in this chapter and Chapter 3. Consider the bolded words in these everyday examples:

Gosh! *Look at the lightning!*
Oh, wow! *This asparagus is delicious.*
Oh no! *We've got a flat tyre!*
Yay! *We've won!*

These are all frequently used in speaking, though we might not write them, especially in formal situations – in informal writing such as friendly emails, text-messages and social media postings, they are often used. Because some were so rare in writing before the era of e-communications, especially in the works of the great literary writers used as models, grammarians just dumped them in a ragbag category of **interjections**, traditionally defined as small words expressing emotional reactions. Many such words show emotional reactions (*wow, gosh, oh no, yippee, heavens, gee, heck*, as well as taboo words).

REFLECTION POINT

These examples of interjections are taken from an English school grammar published in 1887. How many of them have survived till today?

Can you imagine yourself using any of them?

INTERJECTIONS.

EXAMPLES.—OH *no !*   AH! *it was sad.*
HUSH ! *be silent.*   HOY! *come back.*

EXPLANATION.—These words, *Oh ah, hush, hoy*, are called Interjections.

12. An Interjection is a word which ex-presses some feeling or wish ; as, *Ah ! it was very unfortunate.*

EXERCISE IX.

☞ Point out the Interjections :—

Fie ! how could you do so ?   Ah me! it is all over.   Hey-day ! what is the matter ?   Bravo ! my boys.   Hush ! do not make a noise.   Alas ! what have you done !   Heigho ! I am very tired.   Hurrah ! we are to have a holiday.

Figure 4.2 Interjections.
Source: *Grammar for Beginners. Being an Introduction to Allen and Cornwell's English School Grammar.* By the same authors. Simkin, Marshall, & Co.: London. 1887, pp. 17–18.

CONCLUSION

This chapter and Chapter 3 have looked at the different types of words and phrases that act as building blocks in English grammar. Using the grammatical toolbox, we can shape the big blocks and small blocks into patterns and meanings Although we may sometimes think of grammar as an abstract set of rules designed to trip us up, it is much more rewarding to see grammar as a resource for making different kinds of meanings. But the builder still has to decide how to cement everything into place so that it does not fall down or look like a ram-shackle and careless chaos. The most suitable tools have to be chosen and used. Choices have to be made to construct some-thing that makes sense, which says what it wants to say and is comprehensible to the listener or reader.

FURTHER READING

Aarts, B. 2011. *Oxford Modern English Grammar*. **Oxford: Oxford University Press.**
This grammar has natural examples from speaking and writing based on corpus data and other sources. The book takes the description of word classes into much further detail than this basic introduction. Chapter 3 is an informative and thorough description of the word classes and types of phrases.

Carter, R. and M. McCarthy. 2006. *Cambridge Grammar of English*. **Cambridge: Cambridge University Press.**
The sections on word classes (sections 155–66, pages 296–316) give a brief introduction to nouns, verbs, adjectives, adverbs, prepositions and conjunctions, along with the phrases that can be built around them. There then follow more detailed chapters on each of the word classes. As with the rest of the book, Ron Carter and I place the emphasis on corpus evidence.

The Cambridge University Press dictionary website **https://dictionary. cambridge.org/** contains a free, online English grammar. Just click on *Grammar* and you can search for explanations of grammar items and features. The grammar is primarily designed for English as a foreign or second language learners but is useful for anyone wanting to check a standard British English grammar point.

5

THEORIES AND THINKERS

PUTTING THEIR THINKING CAPS ON

Most grammarians have some sort of theory at the back of their minds, and, in some cases, the theory becomes the centre of everything. A theory is a set of ideas that attempt to explain something. For example, astronomers have theorised that there is a big, unknown planet beyond Neptune which could explain certain otherwise inexplicable phenomena in our solar system. We have not discovered the planet, so it remains theoretical. If there turns out to be a different explanation for the unexplained phenomena, then the mystery planet theory may end up being abandoned. A theory of grammar will similarly stand or fall on its ability to explain the phenomena that we can observe in the available data.

Some theories start from the idea that grammar comes from inside of us, that it has something to do with our minds and how the human mind is constructed and operates. Since we are all the same as human beings and different from other animals, it would seem reasonable to see grammar as a property of the human mind, and that, whatever language we speak, there must be some underlying, universal principles at work: a universal grammar. The job of the grammarian, therefore, is to discover the underlying rules and to express them in an abstract form through which the sets of rules for individual languages can be worked out.

However, the human mind is immensely complex. In fact, it is very difficult to separate the idea of our *mind* from the activity of our *brain*. Our brain is in control of mental activity such as perception, memory, attention, problem-solving, psychological states, creative activity and so on. Therefore, what goes on in the world and the meaning of our experiences cannot be divorced from the brain and its activity. The job of the grammarian becomes connecting these activities and meanings with how we express them in language. So, the grammar of a language is not just a set of formal rules but a systematic explanation of the relationship between the grammar, the vocabulary, the **semantics** (the system of meanings) and the human psychology.

For other scholars, grammar is something we 'do' as social animals, rather than something we 'think'. Just as the things we do as humans are varied, and shift and evolve, grammar varies, shifts and evolves to suit our social needs. In this view, the job of the grammarian is to try to explain the relationship between grammar and our social lives in terms of the functions of our experiences. The goal is understanding how actions, experiences and events are expressed socially, who or what is involved in an event, when and where things take place, how certain they are, who is communicating the message to whom, how the message is communicated, and so on. The language is a system of social symbols.

This is quite a crude distinction, and of course there are shades of grey between these different extremes. However, this book is about the basics and we shall concentrate on the most basic ideas.

IT STANDS TO REASON: LOGIC AND RULES

In Chapter 1, we mentioned how for the ancient Greeks and Romans grammar was a set of techniques for effective rhetoric and great literature. This led to the belief, dominant over many centuries right down to our own time, that the great writers and orators were in possession of the best techniques for expressing complex ideas. Modelling grammar on the works of great writers rests upon the theory that good grammar is related to good and rightful thinking and that there are ways of expressing things which are less good. Good thinking depends on the notion of reason, our ability to make decisions and judgements based on facts and logic. It is therefore possible to formulate grammatical rules based on reason and logic.

What's more, if language is seen as a vehicle for clear thinking and reason, then languages which have produced great works of philosophy, history, poetry and drama might well be seen as theoretically superior in some way, and to be the ideal models that other languages should aspire to in writing the rules. If you could show that English could be described in the same way as Latin or ancient Greek, that its grammar was based on the same principles of reason and logic, that its foundations and origins could be traced scientifically to explain its current attributes, your language might be considered a high-quality product. You needed models of correctness from the past and other historical resources to support your theory and to justify the reasoning behind the rules.

Many of the grammars we inherited over the centuries, especially those from the late eighteenth and early nineteenth centuries, the 'age of reason', are marked by this way of thinking. Writing grammar was a scientific undertaking which supported its statements with evidence and reason. The traces of that approach were still apparent in school grammars of the early twentieth century.

INFORMATION ADD-ON

One grammarian of the end of the eighteenth century, Bishop Lowth of Oxford, refers to 'the science of grammar' in the preface to his *Short Introduction to English Grammar*, first published in 1762. This quote comes from the 1799 edition:

> The principal design of a grammar of any language, is to teach us to express ourselves with propriety in that language; and to enable us to judge of every phrase and form of construction, whether it be right or not. The plain way of doing this is, to lay down rules, and to illustrate them by examples.
>
> (Lowth 1762/1799: viii)

Lowth believed that, by learning the rules of English grammar, the student would be better prepared to understand the universal principles of grammar as an aid to learning other languages.

STRUCTURALISM

Another way of looking at grammar is to think of it as a closed system of interrelated parts, rather like what we find if we open up the back of an old pocket watch; all the parts are linked to one another in relationships and purposes that can be mutually defined. The wheels and springs whirr away and the watch ticks without reference to anything outside of it. Similarly, grammar can be seen as internally structured; we can only define one part of the grammar in relation to other parts.

Structuralism, which became influential in America in the first half of the twentieth century, had implications for how a grammar is constructed. An important founding figure in the evolution of structuralism was the Swiss linguist Ferdinand de Saussure (1857–1913). The famous *Cours de linguistique générale* (Course in General Linguistics), based on his lectures, outlined a theory of language as a social phenomenon. He saw languages as a system with an internal structure. Language could either be studied **synchronically** (how it is at one given point in time) or **diachronically** (how it changes over time), but not both at the same time.

Saussure expanded what the linguist should be interested in beyond the world of great literature and writing:

> The subject matter of linguistics comprises all manifestations of human speech, whether that of savages or civilized nations, or of archaic, classical or decadent periods. In each period the linguist must consider not only correct speech and flowery language, but all other forms of expression as well.
>
> (Saussure 1916/2011: 6)

What is special about human language is that it is a 'system of distinct signs corresponding to distinct ideas' (10). When we speak, we act as individuals, but we are using something which is essentially a social object. *Language* is:

> the social side of speech, outside the individual who can never create nor modify it by himself; it exists only by virtue of a sort of contract signed by the members of a community. Moreover, the individual

must always serve an apprenticeship in order to learn the functioning of language; a child assimilates it only gradually.

(Saussure 1916/2011: 14)

Language is a system of arbitrary, conventional signs which mutually define one another. If the system is closed like the machinery of a big old clock, with all the cogs and levers working in collaboration, then we can study it at a given point in its history, and need not concern ourselves with change over time.

If you are studying grammar synchronically, you do not need to concern yourself with the origins of words and you do not need to work out how your grammar relates to other languages, whether Latin or any other. You need to work out what the parts of the machine are through direct observation and then describe how they fit together. Meaning becomes a set of contrasts: An item only 'means' in terms of what it does not mean when put alongside other items in a set. *Took* only has meaning in relation to *take, takes, taking* and *taken.*

Saussure uses the analogy of the chess board (1916/2011: 23). It may be interesting to know the history of chess or what the chess

Figure 5.1 Grammar and the chess board.
Source: Image © M. J. McCarthy 2020.

pieces are made of, but none of that alters the internal consistency of the rules of chess; chess is a closed system, where all the pieces and how they can move relate to one another and to the squares on the board. The chess analogy is a good one for grammar: The pieces are a limited set of items, and their possible moves follow the conventions. Figure 5.1 shows an African chess board, with the king and queen as a lion and lioness. The figures look different from a typical European set with typical European kings and queens and bishops, but the functions and moves of the pieces are the same.

For structuralists, working out how the parts of a language fit together, especially those of newly contacted societies or of languages not previously described, often demands field work, that is to say, embedding oneself in a society and listening, observing and drawing conclusions from all the observable evidence.

The American structural linguist Leonard Bloomfield (1887–1949) was greatly influential in his belief that a language could be studied applying purely empirical methods of observation. In 1933, Bloomfield published his most famous book, *Language*. In it, he says:

> [S]peakers cooperate in a very refined way by means of language signals. In describing a language, we are concerned primarily with the working of this cooperation at any one time in any one community, and not with its occasional failure or with its changes in the course of history.
>
> (Bloomfield 1933/1935: 158)

The linguist observes the forms of language and notices resemblances. We can go from one utterance to another and notice 'partial resemblance' (1933/1935: 159). In a variety of utterances, we can see similarities:

Mary ran
Bill ran
Mary fell   *poor Mary fell*
Bill fell   *poor Bill fell*
Dan fell   *poor Dan fell*

(modelled on Bloomfield 1933/1935: 158–62)

Soon we might hear *Mary sang, Mary danced, Mary laughed*, and *Bill danced, Bill walked, poor Bill danced and fell, the poor man fell*, etc.

In this way it becomes possible to build up a grammar from the smallest units of sound (phonemes) via morphemes and phrases to sentences, without recourse to a complex apparatus of meaning. Meaning, in the sense of complex mental concepts, is in fact so complicated and so dependent on situations and all the possible factors therein, that not much can be achieved by trying to state it. Mental processes are irrelevant to the grammarian. What matters are the similarities and contrasts in form. The constituents of phrases such as *poor John* and *poor Bill* show similarities but also contrast with one another (John and Bill are not the same person). *Poor Bill fell* and *Poor Mary fell* contrast in meaning with one another but are also similar in form (both names can be preceded by *poor* and their word order is similar) and can become constituents in larger units such as sentences.

The structuralist principles of manipulating similarities in form and arrangement working from the smallest units of sound can be seen in the grammars written by scholars such as the British linguist Harold E. Palmer (Palmer 1924) and the American Charles Carpenter Fries (Fries 1945, 1952). Both were reacting against the rule-bound traditional, Latin-based grammars that had dominated in education, and both emphasise the role of phonetics in the learning of the grammar of a language.

Structural grammar was very formal, and structuralist grammarians preferred to work independently of semantics (the meaning system) and the processes of the mind. However, we should not think of structuralism as a theory that only applied to followers of linguists such as Saussure and Bloomfield. The linguist Peter Matthews points out that Saussure and Bloomfield did not themselves talk of 'structuralism' and that many types of grammatical theory are based on ideas about 'structure', the belief that grammar is systematically structured (Matthews 2001: 4). *Structuralism* is more a convenient label for a particular theoretical stance which we can extract from the works of linguists like Saussure and Bloomfield. The remaining theories in this chapter are also concerned with the structure of language, but in quite different ways.

NOAM CHOMSKY AND HIS GRAMMAR

COLOURLESS GREEN IDEAS

In the 1950s, the American linguist Noam Chomsky presented a new theory of grammar which was quite different from the structuralism of the 1930s and 1940s. In the introduction to his famous book *Syntactic Structures* published in 1957, Chomsky states that the purpose of a grammar is to establish a method that will be valid for any language and which will generate *all and only all* of the grammatical sentences of a language and none of the non-grammatical ones. By *grammatical* sentences, Chomsky means sentences judged by a native speaker of a language to conform to the rules. The sentence *Colourless green ideas sleep furiously* is not something we can easily imagine as happening, but, even so, it follows the rules of the *grammar* of English sentences (noun phrase + verb phrase + adverbial phrase). On the other hand, the sentence *Furiously sleep ideas green colourless* is meaningless *and* ungrammatical (Chomsky 1957: 15). The grammar is *formal*: it is concerned with the rules for arranging the forms of sentences, rather than describing how they relate to meanings in the world.

What we know about the grammar of our language as native speakers is independent of what we know about the vocabulary or about the world. The rules are abstract and, underlying them are principles that apply to all languages.

Chomsky shows how a sentence can be expressed as a **phrase structure**. The phrase structure shows the underlying structure of the sentence, how each part is related to the others in building up what we see or hear on the 'surface'. The sentence *The engineers examined the bridge* can be built up from a core structure of noun phrase + verb phrase, step-by-step. *NP* means noun phrase, *VP* means verb phrase, which here includes the verb phrase and the noun phrase acting as object (which some grammarians call the predicate) and *(DET)* means determiner (e.g. *the, this, my*):

Sentence
NP + VP
(DET) + NP + VP
(DET) + NP + Verb + NP
The + N + Verb + NP
The + engineers + Verb + NP
The + engineers + examined + NP
The + engineers + examined + (DET) + NP
The + engineers + examined + the + N
The + engineers + examined + the + bridge

(after Chomsky 1957: 27)

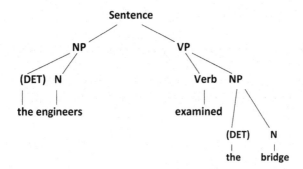

Figure 5.2 Tree-diagram of sentence structure.

Each line after the first represents the application of a rule and each line 'rewrites' the line before until we reach the actual sentence: the **surface structure**. The same sentence structure can be drawn as a tree-diagram (Figure 5.2).

The tree-diagram helps us to see the structure more clearly. It shows us, for instance, that *the bridge* is a component of the structure, but *examined the* or *the examined* are not, because they belong to different branches of the tree.

TRANSFORMATIONS

One of the questions Chomsky raises in his 1957 book is the connection between active and passive voice sentences. With our example above, *the engineers examined the bridge*, if we change it around to *the bridge examined the engineers*, it no longer makes sense. But it does make sense and means more or less the same as the original if we say *the bridge was examined by the engineers*.

Chomsky concludes that there are certain obligatory changes that are necessary to produce the grammatically correct passive voice sentence. We have to use an auxiliary or modal verb (in this case *was*) and the past participle of the verb (in this case *examined*). These obligatory changes are rules which allow us to transform the active voice sentence into an equivalent passive voice one which is grammatically correct – they are 'grammatical transformations' (Chomsky 1957: 44). Chomsky's theory became known as **transformational grammar**.

However, we do not *have* to use the passive voice. It is a choice. Passive voice sentences are transformations of underlying, core, active voice sentences which are like the kernels of nuts, the innermost part hidden under the outer shell. Chomsky refers to *kernel sentences*, which are simple, declarative, active voice sentences with no complex verb or noun phrases: 'Thus every sentence of the language will either belong to the kernel or will be derived from the strings underlying one or more kernel sentences by a sequence of one or more transformations' (Chomsky 1957: 45).

Once we have stated the phrase structure rules for kernel sentences, all other grammatically correct sentences can be created by transformations.

Transformational grammar is a formal grammar. Trying to include statements about meaning is 'relatively useless' (Chomsky 1957: 101).

Figure 5.3 The outer shell and the kernel.
Source: Image © M. J. McCarthy 2020.

FROM THE DEPTHS TO THE SURFACE

Chomsky's next major work was *Aspects of the Theory of Syntax* (Chomsky 1965). In this book, Chomsky says the job of the grammarian is to get at what speakers of a language know about their language. The target is:

> an ideal speaker-listener, in a completely homogeneous speech community, who knows its language perfectly and is unaffected by such grammatically irrelevant conditions as memory limitations, distractions, shifts of attention and interest, and errors (random or characteristic) in applying his knowledge of the language in actual performance.
>
> (Chomsky 1965: 3)

The idea of 'actual performance' is important here: How we use our language in real situations, with all the slips, hesitations, mistakes and lack of attention is not the same as our knowledge of the language. **Performance** in a language is not the same as **competence**; competence is our underlying knowledge of the language. Performance is a type of behaviour. For Chomsky, behaviour was like circus animals getting rewards for acting in a certain way, and he was very critical of the behavioural psychologist B. F. Skinner and his book *Verbal Behavior* (Skinner 1957). For Chomsky, language was not at all like animals responding to external stimuli and rewards in the environment: 'there must be fundamental processes at work quite independently of "feedback" from the environment' (Chomsky 1959: 42).

The grammarian must look deep into the human mind for the universal principles which enable us to understand and create new, well-formed sentences we have never heard or seen before. And the evidence is there before our eyes, in the way children learn their language: 'The fact that all normal children acquire essentially comparable grammars of great complexity with remarkable rapidity suggests that human beings are somehow specially designed to do this' (Chomsky 1959: 57).

In another work he says: 'a grammar is not a description of the performance of the speaker, but rather of his linguistic competence … a description of competence and a description of performance are different things' (Chomsky 1964: 35).

It is not enough to just describe the surface structure and its related parts as the earlier structuralists did or as traditional grammarians did. Traditional grammars, even though they give rules, fail to bring to light the underlying principles which enable us to create an infinite number of sentences which a native speaker of the language would recognise as correct. Below the surface of performance there are principles for generating well-formed sentences and the principles underlying kernel sentences are likely to be universal. Transformations enable us to get from the **deep structure** to **the surface structure**.

What is needed, according to Chomsky, is a grammar which shows how we generate all those possible sentences. So, the grammar should be a **transformational-generative grammar**.

Chomsky's theory was influential in America amongst linguists, and influenced the way children's grammar was studied, as well as how the acquisition of second languages was investigated. However, it is not likely that you will see a strong fingerprint of transformational-generative grammar in school textbooks or the national curriculums for English in English-speaking countries. A lot of Chomsky's theory remained just that – theory, and he never claimed that his way of looking at grammar had a direct application in grammar teaching.

BEARING EVERYTHING IN MIND: COGNITIVE GRAMMAR

THE MIND AND THE WORLD

Cognitive grammar, as the name suggests, is concerned with the relationship between the activities of the human mind in relation to the world and our experiences, and how grammar reflects them. This is different from Chomsky's concern with the human mind as possessing the capacity to recognise in different languages the underlying universal principles of grammaticality. Cognitive grammar came to the fore in the late 1970s and 1980s. It is most closely associated with the theories of the American linguist Ronald Langacker.

Although *cognitive grammar* might sound a little like an exploration of the human mind similar to that which Chomsky carried out, it is very different. Langacker describes his cognitive approach to language in the following way:

> A cognitive approach to language can also be a pragmatic approach, for cognition figures crucially in linguistic behavior, social interaction, and contextual understanding. Despite its emphasis on conceptualization (broadly understood as encompassing all mental experience), cognitive grammar explicitly denies the existence of any sharp or specific boundary between pragmatic and linguistic considerations.
>
> (Langacker 2009: 78)

Langacker specifically excludes from cognitive grammar 'the derivation of surface forms from underlying structures' (2009: 79). What matters is our experience, and our experience repeats itself in events which enable us to create mental schemas or *frames* for the events, and such schemas are conventionally established in speech communities. For example, we have an idea of what is involved in a typical exchange of goods in a shop, that it involves money, goods, a buyer, paying, etc. (Schmid and Ungerer 2011).

Cognitive grammar brings together the world, the set of symbols that language offers us and our mental representations of the world. As Vyvyan Evans and Melanie Green put it, 'Language offers a window into cognitive function, providing insights into the nature, structure and organisation of thoughts and ideas' (Evans and Green 2015: 5).

SYMBOLS AND CONCEPTS

Language enables us to 'encode' our thoughts and ideas through symbolic forms – in the case of grammar, through the morphemes, words, phrases, etc. The forms are symbolic because they are paired with meanings, just as all symbols are. If you click on a heart shape in response to a social media posting, you are using a symbol (♥ = love). What we perceive in the world is conceptualised in meanings and expressed through the symbolic forms of language. If someone says *the field was full of sunflowers* we have a concept of a field of sunflowers in our mind, maybe a typical one, a stereotype of a field and of a sunflower, or some we have seen – it does not have to be a literal image of the same field the speaker was talking about, or the exact, identical image that is present in the speaker's mind, nor can it be.

Cognitive linguists consider the role played by our knowledge of the world as important. If I have no idea what a sunflower is, I will have difficulty in matching the symbol (the word) and its meaning. Words like *field, was, full, sunflower* have conventional meanings that evoke frames, and, as a speaker of English I will have heard them enough times to be able to relate them to concepts and to have mental images of what the speaker is getting at based on my knowledge of the world (Langacker 1987: ch. 1). Also, it is likely that the sunflowers will be in the foreground of my mind rather than, say, the hedges or fences around the field or the sky above it. The sunflowers are the *figure*; the hedges, fences and sky are the *ground*. Think of it like a portrait of a person in a room: The room is just a background to the main figure, the portrait.

Naturally, both parties in the conversation have to be on the same wavelength; language serves an interactive function. What

Figure 5.4 Imaging the sunflowers.
Source: Image © M. J. McCarthy 2020.

the speaker says must fit with the listener's perception, memories and world knowledge to make much sense.

Cognitive grammar is not just concerned with the unique human faculty of judging whether something is grammatical or not but is interested in the psychological and cultural foundations of how grammar achieves communication. Perception, attention and memory are not 'extras' appended on to how we communicate; they are not just 'performance' features, they are an essential part of the communication of meanings. Grammar is not an abstract set of universal rules; it reflects our experience of the world and contributes to how we shape the world conceptually.

CONSTRUCTIONS

An important feature of cognitive grammar is the idea of **constructions**, which are conventionally understood strings of words. Langacker says:

> Grammar resides in patterns – represented by constructional schemas – for constructing symbolically complex expressions. A typical construction consists of two component symbolic structures that are integrated, both semantically and phonologically, to form a composite symbolic structure.
>
> (Langacker 2009: 83)

Many such strings will be more, or less fixed. The words and phrases in them are not so much 'building blocks' for building structures (Langacker 2009: 84); they are more like prompts or cues to conceptual understandings. Some are very idiomatic, such as when someone says *I got the wrong end of the stick* (meaning they misinterpreted a situation); we can neither change the words (*I got the wrong end of the pole*) nor the word order (*the wrong end of the stick was what I got*) without changing the meaning or creating a string of words that make little or no sense, or introducing absurdity into the conversation.

On the other hand, a construction need not be idiomatic in the way *get the wrong end of the stick* is. These sentences share the same pattern of construction:

I got a shock.
I got the bus.
I got three apples.
I got my diploma.

All three evoke 'things that relate to the speaker' and 'pastness' in our minds but three different types of experience (having a sudden negative experience, boarding a bus, buying or picking apples, receiving or achieving a diploma). *Three* evokes the concept of number; *my* evokes ownership; *the* projects a notion of shared understanding. These are grammatical meanings but they operate in the same way as the vocabulary (*shock, bus, apple, diploma*) in terms of conceptualisation and our experience of the world. We have mental frames for filling in the details of catching buses, picking apples, getting diplomas, etc. which the grammar triggers or prompts. Grammar, vocabulary and meaning all go hand in hand and cannot be separated in an arbitrary fashion (Langacker 1987: 3). Corpora can help us get at the most common constructions that reflect our basic experiences, for example the frame of *cause and receive*, where corpora show that 'the verb attracted most strongly by the cause-receive construction is *give*, followed by *tell, send, offer* and *show*' (Schmid and Ungerer 2011: 620).

USE IT AND NEVER LOSE IT

The more our experience repeats itself, the more often we use common constructions, the frequency of use in itself *becomes* the grammar, rather than the grammar existing abstractly as something taken down from the shelf to use. The structure of grammar emerges from its use, not vice-versa. The more children can hear the language used to refer to basic, common frames, the more they can use it themselves and produce new utterances based on what they regularly hear (Tomasello 2003). This is **usage-based** grammar. Two scholars who have written about cognitive linguistics, William Croft and Allan Cruse, refer to usage-based theory in this way: 'knowledge of language emerges from language use. That is, categories and structures in semantics, syntax, morphology and phonology are built up from our cognition of specific utterances on specific occasions of use' (Croft and Cruse 2004: 4).

In this theoretical perspective, we acquire our grammar by working out, from myriad experiences of hearing the utterances people make to communicate their experiences, how it all works conventionally. And it flows from this that grammar emerges from how people *use* words, rather than being pre-ordained as a set of rules. Furthermore, since grammar never stands still and is always in the middle of the process of 'emerging', we can think of grammar as **emergent**, the approach adopted by the linguist Paul Hopper (Hopper 1996, 2011). *Emergent* captures both the idea of a process which is always ongoing and one which gives rise to unpredictable events (the word *emergent* is used in this way in evolutionary science). The statement that grammar is always on the move echoes Joan Bybee's comment that language is 'more like sand dunes than like a planned structure, such as a building' (Bybee 2010: 2).

This would seem to question the idea of describing grammar as building blocks that come together to form a system. Is grammar just a multitude of fragmented and scattered grains of sand blown about in the wind? The next group of linguists we look at did not think so. They believed that grammar has internal consistency and is a mutually supporting and collaborating system of elements that relate to our social experience.

OUT OF THE MIND: NEO-FIRTHIANS

GRAMMAR AND CONTEXT

Chomsky's theory was a grammar of the mind; competence belonged in the human mental apparatus. The next theory that we examine is one that takes us out of the mind and into the social world. It builds a description of grammar on the relationships between form, function, meaning and context.

The anthropologist Bronisław Malinowski (1884–1942) claimed that 'an utterance has no meaning except in the context of situation' (Malinowski 1923: 307). What we say and write and how it becomes meaningful in context is central to the theory put forward by the British linguist John Rupert Firth (1890–1960), who was influenced by Malinowski's ideas. Firth's pupils and followers became known as the neo-Firthians and their approach to grammar is firmly rooted in social contexts.

For J. R. Firth, everything from the sounds we use in speech (the **phonology** of the language) and the writing system (the **orthography**) are related to the lexis, morphology and syntax, which in turn are related to texts in their contexts (who produces them, when, why, how, etc.) and the wider social situation (Palmer 1968: 175–6). They are like the instruments and sections of an orchestra all playing together in harmony to produce a symphony of meaning. To understand the music completely, you have to listen to what all the players are doing. What matters is the **context of situation**. The central features of the context of situation are the participants and the processes and events in which they engage (which are the same that we used in Chapter 2 when describing English clauses).

A good example of this theory in action is a study carried out by the linguist Terence Mitchell. He researched how people use language when buying and selling at markets and shops in Cyrenaica (part of modern-day Libya). Different aspects of the context of situation (different participants, different settings, etc) influenced the language used. Mitchell identified stages in the commercial exchanges. He observed each consecutive stage:

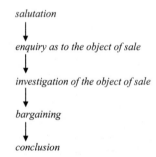

salutation

↓

enquiry as to the object of sale

↓

investigation of the object of sale

↓

bargaining

↓

conclusion

Each stage had differences in languages associated with it. The language varied according to whether the events took place in a shop or a market, whether the markets were open-air or closed markets, what kinds of exchanges the participants were engaged in, their social identities, etc. Mitchell's view was that 'meaning must be sought in use' (Mitchell 1957: 32). This philosophy underpinned the neo-Firthian way of thinking about grammar.

MICHAEL HALLIDAY

One of J. R. Firth's pupils, the British linguist Michael Halliday, did not make the traditional separation of lexis and grammar in his approach to language, and he suggested instead the term *lexico-grammar* (Halliday 1996: 4) as a midway level between the sound and writing systems on one hand and context on the other. The idea that lexis and grammar, as we have understood them so far, might be intimately intertwined was to be reinforced much later when corpora came onto the scene (see Chapter 6).

Halliday was also concerned with structure, in the sense that his theory rested on the concept of closed systems, an idea he put forward in one of his first major articles on grammar (Halliday 1961: 246–7). A closed system consists of a set of mutually exclusive items which define one another's meaning. In the English demonstrative set consisting of *this, that, these, those, this* means 'not *that* or *these* or *those*', and vice-versa, *these* means 'not this, that or those'. You choose to use one member of the system by excluding the others: We can say *this car* or *that car*, but not *★this that car*. If we invent a new piece to add to the chess board, we change the whole game and alter all the internal relations among the chess pieces.

Halliday's 1961 paper is called 'Categories of the Theory of Grammar'. Units of language (e.g. morphemes, words, phrases) form structures, which belong to a hierarchy. As we go up the hierarchy, each class is composed of units from the level immediately below. This is what Halliday calls a *rank scale* (1961: 251). In Figure 5.5, the levels in bold are what we have considered as the limits of grammar in this book. In Chapter 2 we built up a similar rank-scale for grammar level by level, though we used the term *phrase* where Halliday refers to *group*. Meanwhile, the levels in brackets take us beyond sentences into the world of discourse (texts, conversations, etc.), and at the same time can take us below the morpheme into syllables and sounds and letters and the actions of speaking and writing.

FUNCTIONS AND SYSTEMS

The clause is at the centre of Halliday's grammar. That is where we see subject (S), predicator (i.e. verb) (P), complement (C) and

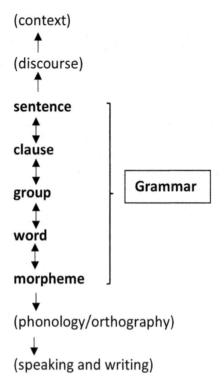

Figure 5.5 Rank scale.

adjunct (A) working together to express the roles of the participants in the clause (S and C), the processes (P) and the circumstances (A) (Halliday 1967: 39). In Chapter 2, we used slightly different labels (S, V, O, C and A) but the grammatical description there roughly followed Halliday's principles. SVOCA are not just formal, abstract labels like NP and VP in Chomsky's grammar; they refer to **clause functions**, what each element is *doing* in the clause.

The idea of systems is important in Halliday's grammar. Once we enter a system, each choice presents us with further choices, and each choice is an *entry condition* to the next set of choices (Halliday 1967). Figure 5.6 shows a system network based on the subject personal pronouns for referring to humans (*I, you, he, she, we, they,* but excluding pronoun *one*):

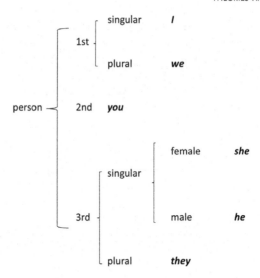

Figure 5.6 Personal pronouns system: Human subjects.

In Figure 5.6, if we choose a first-person pronoun, we then must choose if it is singular *I* or plural *we*. Second-person *you* is the same for singular and plural in English, so there is no choice to be made. If we choose third person and choose singular, we must then choose between *he* and *she* to refer to a male or female person. The female/male choice does not apply to plural third-person subjects in English.

Other languages will have different systems with different choices. Spanish not only distinguishes between *you* in the singular and *you* in the plural, but the speaker must also make the choice as to whether it is a respectful 'distant' *you* (e.g. a person you don't know, a person in authority) or a close, intimate *you* (e.g. a member of your family or a friend).

Because of the emphasis on systems and on the functions of the various grammatical units such as subjects and objects, Halliday's grammar is known as a **systemic-functional grammar**.

GRAMMAR IN SOCIETY

In 1978, Halliday published a book called *Language as Social Semiotic* which links features of language form to aspects of meaning and context, just as J. R. Firth had done. Halliday refers to three features of the context, what he calls the *field, tenor* and *mode* (Halliday 1978):

- Field: The content or argument of a text.
- Tenor: The relationship between the speaker/writer and the listener/reader.
- Mode: The channel of communication (e.g. speech or writing).

These features of context root the grammar firmly in society rather than seeing grammar as a mental construct. The field connects with choices of how to express the various relationships between the SVOCA elements of clauses (who is doing what in the world), the tenor will affect choices such as whether to make a statement or ask a question, or whether to use a tentative modal verb, the mode will raise choices of how to organise the information (e.g. using a fronted adverbial or linking expressions). It is this socially rooted approach to grammar which I have followed in this book and you will have recognised that much of Chapters 2, 3 and 4 are written in the spirit of Firth and Halliday's grammatical theory.

CONCLUSION: THEORY AND THEORIES

In this chapter we have looked at grammar not as a set of rules for English but more as a human phenomenon that could have a variety of different explanations. Possible explanations are moulded into theories. Theories always need to be tested against available data. Think of a theory as one of those ancient maps of the world, made when mapmakers had not travelled around the globe. They theorised and imagined what the remotest parts must be like. Ancient maps often made it look as though the world was flat, and that you could sail off the edge of it if you were not careful, and there were huge monsters to contend with if you strayed into the unknown regions. As we gathered more data, especially as scientific knowledge increased, and aerial photography was invented, we understood better how the planet was shaped, and we changed the map of the world to what we have today.

Grammatical theories have changed over the centuries, and like any theories, they vary depending on the nature of what is taken

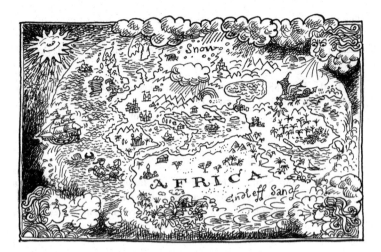

Figure 5.7 Mapping the unknown.
Source: © Jake Tebbit 2020.

into account. The science of the mind and the brain and the science of society have all contributed to how grammatical theory is framed. This *basics* book cannot possibly do more than give you a flavour of the wide range of theories, and it only covers a few of the main and most influential ones.

There will always be new ways of looking at data, and different types of data will become available on which to base new theories. Corpora and corpus software, for example, give us access to volumes of data which would be far too big for any individual to read and investigate manually, and we shall see more of that and how it affects our ideas about grammar in the next chapter.

Data and observation enable us to refine theory, but one truth remains: If your map and the place you are mapping turn out to be different and contradict each other, it is the map which is wrong.

FURTHER READING

Graffi, G. 2005. 20th century linguistics: Overview of trends. In K. Brown (ed.), *Encyclopedia of Language and Linguistics*. 2nd edition. Oxford: Elsevier Science, 181–195.

This article covers all the major theories of twentieth-century linguistics and pays special attention to structuralism and generative grammar. It includes an introduction to Ferdinand de Saussure's work and further discussion of J. R. Firth's ideas.

Radford, A. 1988. *Transformational Grammar: A First Course.* **Cambridge: Cambridge University Press.**
This is a clear introduction to the complexities of transformational grammar which takes things further than the rough sketch in this chapter has been able to. All the central terminology of transformational grammar is explained in a very accessible style.

Ungerer, F. and Schmid, H.-J. 2006. *An Introduction to Cognitive Linguistics.* **2nd edition. Harlow: Pearson Longman.**
This gives an introduction to the major concepts in cognitive linguistics. It covers areas such as the role of prototypes and metaphors, as well as taking further the main concepts outlined in this chapter.

Halliday, M. A. K. 1978. *Language as Social Semiotic: The Social Interpretation of Language and Meaning.* **London: Edward Arnold.**
This book gives important background to Michael Halliday's way of thinking about language in general and about grammar. It shows how the system of *lexicogrammar* relates to features of register and the system of meanings in social contexts.

6

WORD OF MOUTH
GRAMMAR IN ACTION

IN A MANNER OF SPEAKING

The grammar we built in Chapters 2, 3 and 4 will, unless otherwise stated, suffice for both speaking and writing. We have only occasionally shown how different grammar can be in speaking compared with writing (e.g. the graphs on *whom* and on sentence linking in Chapter 2 and Chapter 4).

In my 1998 book on spoken language, I said this about grammar:

> Spoken grammar must always be elaborated in its own terms, using spoken data. If, at the end of the exercise, spoken and written are shown to have many features in common, then this is a convenience to be thankful for, and not something that can be prejudged without careful research. Our task is to identify precisely those areas which are shared and those which are not.
>
> (McCarthy, 1998: 90)

There is no doubt that the grammars of speaking and writing share a great deal. The linguist Geoffrey Leech suggested it was better to think of the whole of English grammar conforming to a general, underlying system but varying in its specific applications in speaking and writing and in different registers within speaking and writing (Leech 2000).

Writing is important; it is a way of storing our knowledge and experience outside of our human bodies; written documents have been handed down from generation to generation. Many societies have also achieved the passing on of knowledge through oral transmission, but writing has allowed humans to record immense complexity in thought and science. In this chapter, however, we pay specific attention to grammar in speaking. This is because speech is primary – all human societies use it, and many human languages have existed either without a writing system or with one borrowed from some other language.

INFORMATION ADD-ON

Leonard Bloomfield (see Chapter 5) made the following observation:

> Writing is not language, but merely a way of recording language by means of visible marks. In some countries, such as China, Egypt, and Mesopotamia, writing was practised thousands of years ago, but to most of the languages that are spoken today it has been applied either in relatively recent times or not at all. Moreover, until the days of printing, literacy was confined to a very few people. All languages were spoken through nearly all of their history by people who did not read or write; the languages of such peoples are just as stable, regular, and rich as the languages of literate nations.

> (Bloomfield 1933/1935: 21)

Consider a normal day and how much more speaking than writing is involved in getting through the day. If we take a word-count of a typical corpus of everyday, informal English conversations among friends, family and acquaintances, we find that, on average, people talk at a rate of 100 or more words per minute. You only have to chat with someone for half an hour for the two of you to produce more than 3,000 words. How many times do you write 3,000 words per day? If I could do that, I would have had this book finished in three weeks instead of six months.

There is every good reason for looking closely at the grammar of informal speaking, since that is what most people do with language most of the time. Here are some of the reasons for investigating spoken grammar:

- Over the centuries, grammatical descriptions and prescriptions were dominated by the study of writing, especially the writing of the great and the good, the authors of the English national literary canon such as William Shakespeare and John Milton. That is not surprising since it is only relatively recently that we have been able to record sound and to 'freeze' the spoken language.

- With the power of corpus-analytical software, and providing we can transcribe audio recordings into a computer-readable form of text (no mean feat, and something that at present consumes hours of human labour), we can investigate massive amounts of data at the click of a mouse in ways that would have taken years to do manually, to make comparisons between the grammar of speaking and the grammar of writing.

- It is in speech that we see the greatest differences in dialects and varieties of English. When we write English formally, we tend towards the educated standard, so that there will be little difference in the writing produced by academics and professionals who use English around the world, whatever distinctive variety they may use in their everyday speech. An academic from Belfast in Northern Ireland may speak English differently from an academic from Birmingham in England, a business person from Malaysia may speak English differently from a Nigerian business person, but when they write their books and articles and proposals and reports, they normally use a shared, international educated/professional standard English grammar.

- The distinctiveness of dialects and varieties, how they emerge and evolve, arise from contact between languages, migrations of people, international commerce and cooperation, conquest and colonisation, and the spread of the media. The way dialects and varieties develop and change does not happen through laziness or poor education. It is a natural, organic process; grammar is always 'on the move'. It never stands still, even though we may notice it changing far less than our ever-changing vocabulary, where new words crowd into the dictionary every year.

SPEAKING AND WRITING: A GRAMMAR FOR EVERY OCCASION

Chapters 2, 3 and 4 were based on a standard grammar that does not single out special features either of speaking or writing, except where they are most noticeably different. But grammar is not some great monolith and the way we write has its own different uses of grammar (e.g. academic writing compared with a friendly email), as does the way we speak (e.g. a story told in a rural dialect versus a formal university lecture).

Comparisons between spoken and written corpora have enabled us to observe grammatical features which offer new ways of describing spoken grammar. Consider these observations which corpora have enabled us to make:

- Grammar in informal speaking has features which are not found in formal writing.
- Some common items of informal spoken grammar are rare in formal writing, and vice-versa.
- Some items which are found in both speaking and writing have different meanings and functions.
- Some features of the grammar of informal speaking push us to rethink the terminology we have come to rely on in describing the standard written grammar of sentences.

The next sections will consider how some of these points can be observed in everyday speaking.

YOU THINKING WHAT I'M THINKING?

If you think about grammar and how you chat informally in English with friends and family, you may conclude that the description of the SVOCA clause elements outlined in Chapter 2 all fit together in a suspiciously neat and tidy way. In everyday spoken English, you will not have to wait long to hear things like:

You talking to me?
Got a pen I can borrow?
Can't stand those TV reality shows!

Lost his job, did he?
No, didn't hear a thing. Sorry. Happened in the night, did it?

The feature which these examples have in common is called
ellipsis. Ellipsis refers to things which, according to the conventions of formal writing we would expect to be present but, for one
reason or another, are not. We might 'rewrite' the examples as:

[Are] you talking to me?
[Have you] got a pen I can borrow?
[I] can't stand those TV reality shows!
[He] lost his job, did he?
No, [I] didn't hear a thing. [I'm] sorry. [It] happened in the night, did it?

'Rewrite' is in quote marks, and that is deliberate because that is
what we would be doing – creating written versions of sentences
which were not what the speaker said. The words in square
brackets are not 'missing' in any way, though you might expect to
find them in more formal conversations or in formal, written
documents.

In conversation, speakers understand one another with no difficulty whatsoever when they hear utterances like our examples.
Randolph Quirk and his co-authors, in their *Comprehensive Grammar of the English Language*, call this *situational* ellipsis (Quirk et al.
1985: 895–6). We understand the words in square brackets in the
examples because they are obvious in the context and simply do
not need to be said. This feature of 'not stating the obvious' is
most common at the beginning of an utterance and when it is
pronouns and auxiliary verb meanings that are obvious, but it can
also happen in with definite or indefinite articles:

Hurry up! Bus is coming! [the bus]
A: You looking for something? [Are you looking …]
B: Screwdriver. Can't find one anywhere. [A screwdriver. I can't find
one …]

Situational ellipsis often happens when people are doing jobs
together such as cooking, repairing things or moving furniture,
where everything is visible and obvious in the context (see the

examples in Carter and McCarthy 1997). Ellipsis is a common feature of informal spoken grammar. Instead of saying it dispenses with stating the obvious, or that it is a 'reduced' grammar, it makes equal sense to say that writing usually spells things out more because most written documents are not read at the moment they are produced but at a time when the writer and reader are in a different time and place.

THIS BOOK, YOU NEVER KNOW WHAT IT'S GOING TO SAY NEXT ...

HEADS OR TAILS?

If someone you know well said, 'that woman who works in the shop, her husband, his car got stolen last night', you would prob-ably have enough information to know just who was being talked about and what had happened. However, if we try to analyse the utterance in terms of the SVOCA clause elements we are likely to get into a fix:

S   V   A

That woman who works in the shop, her husband, <u>his car got stolen last night</u>.

We have identified S, V and A but we seem to have a lot of material left over. We assume that *his* refers to the husband and the woman who works in the shop is his wife. But where does this information fit into the conventions of the clause? It doesn't. All the words before the subject *his car* are a sort of headline or **header** like the header in an email telling you the topic of the email. We could rewrite the utterance so that it becomes like the set of nested Russian dolls on p. 47:

The car belonging to husband of the woman who works in the shop got stolen.

or as:

The woman who works in the shop's husband's car got stolen.

To my mind, neither of these alternative versions is as natural, or as listener-friendly as the original one. Headers are useful in conversation: Speakers provide listeners with the information they need, often like a series of stepping-stones from what the listener knows to the news they don't know (you know the woman, you know she has a husband, you won't be surprised that he has a car, but, news – it was stolen!).

Another type of information that lies outside of the clause can be seen in the words in bold in this example from the grammar I wrote with Ronald Carter:

> **He's** amazingly clever, **that dog of theirs**.
>
> (Carter and McCarthy 2006: 194)

Here we seem to have two subjects: *that dog of theirs* 'fills out' *he*. In our corpus research, Ron Carter and I found that this kind of construction, which we called a **tail** (in contrast to a header, because it's tacked on to the end), was common when speakers were giving an opinion or judging something. We chose the terms *headers* and *tails* as they are more transparent and memorable than terms such as *left-dislocation* (headers) and *right-dislocation* (tails) which other linguists have used. Nothing is 'dislocated', and speaking doesn't have a left and right; that metaphor is taken from the way western languages are written on the page (McCarthy and Carter 1997; McCarthy 1998: 60–2). It is often necessary to rethink some of our terminology if we want to be faithful to the spoken language that we use every day.

PRONOUNS, THEY WORK HARD, THEY DO

Just as we can do things with nouns at the beginning and end of the clause, we can repeat a pronoun subject using a pronoun and a repeated or substituted verb in the tail:

*Lawrence, **he's** crazy **he is**.*
*I'm thirsty, **I am**.*

Ron Carter and I, in our 2006 grammar, give more examples of headers and tails (Carter and McCarthy 2006: 192–6). They are an illustration of how grammar in informal speaking is assembled linearly, step-by-step (Brazil 1995).

REFLECTION POINT

Compare the different effects of alternative ways of saying the following:

a   *A friend of mine, her father runs an online legal advice company.*
b   *A friend of mine's father runs an online legal advice company.*
c   *The father of a friend of mine runs an online legal advice company.*

a   *I'm so forgetful.*
b   *I'm so forgetful, I am.*
c   *I'm so forgetful, me.*
d   *Me, I'm so forgetful.*
e   *Myself, I'm so forgetful.*

a   *Those flowers are amazing.*
b   *They're amazing, those flowers.*
c   *Those flowers, they're amazing.*

MARK MY WORDS

Other words seem to fall outside the clause structure too. Some common expressions in everyday speaking monitor the state of shared knowledge between the speakers, that is to say the extent to which speakers can or can't assume that they and their listener(s) are on the same wavelength. English provides us with expressions such as *you know* (generally speaking, you and I are on the same wavelength), *you see* (I can't assume we're on the same wavelength, so I'm telling you this) and *I mean* (I think I need to elaborate more). All three expressions look like subjects followed by transitive verbs (i.e. verbs that normally take an object), yet they frequently appear in contexts where there is no obvious object in the conventional sense:

*I bought it mostly because it was cheap, **you know**.*
*He wasn't invited to the wedding. **You see**, he's not a real cousin of hers, just a distant relative really.*
*It's a complete mystery. **I mean, you know**, why would anyone do that?*

In these examples, there are various positions which you *know, you see* and *I mean* could occupy; they are not fixed:

*I bought it, **you know**, mostly because it was cheap.*
*I bought it mostly because it was, **you know**, cheap.*

Here are some more words (in bold) that seem to be outside of the clause structure.

a   **So**, *let's get started.*
b   **Well**, *shall we stop now?*
c   A: *It's a real shame!*
    B: **Absolutely**.
d   A: *I've had a word with Alice.*
    B: **Right**.
e   A: *I got the job!*
    B: **Brilliant!**

So and *well* in (a) and (b) seem to be marking a boundary, either to starting a new activity or phase in the conversation or ending one. The speakers could also have said *Right* or *Okay*, with more or less the same meaning. In (c), *definitely* or *totally* could have been used with a similar effect. *Right* in (d) seems to be acknowledging 'message received and understood'; speaker B could have said *okay, fine, uhuh, good* or a combination of these words. In (e), *amazing, great, fantastic* would serve equally well.

Although some of the words and the possible alternatives look as if they fall into traditional word classes of adjective (*great, amazing*, etc.) or adverb (*well, absolutely*), they seem to be behaving in a different way from how they behave within clauses; they are responding to what has just been said by someone else or marking some kind of boundary. And the two-word expressions which look like subjects with transitive verbs (*you know, I see*) can float around in different positions without any obvious grammatical object.

For this reason, linguists prefer to think of all of these expressions as **pragmatic markers**, that is, they either mark the listener's personal stance, attitude or reaction, which we call **response tokens** (McCarthy 2002, 2003), or else they mark stages in the speaker's perception of how the conversation is unfolding, which we call **discourse markers** (Schiffrin 1987). Just as the linking expressions in Chapter 2 marked relationships across sentences in writing, pragmatic markers can indicate relationships across utterances and across different speakers. When we take part in informal conversations, we do not speak in 'sentences' in the conventional sense. The discourse markers and the pragmatic markers in (a) to (e) above are part of a grammar of speaking. We need to think in a different way, beyond and outside of the notion of sentences.

REFLECTION POINT

One linguist, David Brazil, in writing about the grammar of speaking, said, 'we do not necessarily have to assume that the consideration of such abstract notions as "sentences" enters into the user's scheme of things at all' (Brazil 1995: 15).

Another linguist, Paul Hopper, is even more dismissive of the concept of the 'sentence': 'It seems to me, and it has seemed so to others also, that the sentence is an artifact of some historical accidents, including most prominently the Western rhetorical and grammatical tradition and the development of a written language' (Hopper 1988: 19).

As with so many other aspects of grammar, the way speakers use pragmatic markers, especially if they are judged to be 'sloppy' or 'overused', can irritate people and generate controversy. It is difficult to describe English grammar coldly and neutrally; it is a minefield of potential public disgruntlement. Almost everyone has an attitude towards grammar and what they consider 'good' or 'bad'. As the main stakeholders in the grammatical marketplace, everyone wants their voices heard.

TAKING CHUNKS OUT OF THE LANGUAGE

Corpus linguists have shown us not only how frequent the individual words of English are, but also how words congeal into frequently repeated chunks. Chunks are strings of words (typically between two and four or five words) which are repeated over and over again in language use. They are particularly common in everyday conversation. We would never be able to speak fluently if we had to assemble every single word afresh each time we opened our mouths. If we couldn't call on a 'dictionary' of ready-made chunks already stored in our memories and immediately retrievable, we would sound a bit like primitive robots. As the linguist Joan Bybee puts it:

> The principal experience that triggers chunking is repetition. If two or more smaller chunks occur together with some degree of frequency, a larger chunk containing the smaller ones is formed. Chunking is of course a property of both production and perception and contributes significantly to fluency and ease in both modes.
>
> (Bybee 2010: 34)

One of the discourse markers we looked at in the previous section, *you know*, is by far the most frequent combination of two words in the Spoken BNC2014 corpus. It occurs more than 45,000 times, and some of its near neighbours in the frequency list of pairs of words include *I think*, which occurs more than 35,000 times, and *I mean*, which occurs almost 20,000 times. If we up our game and get the computer to find longer chunks of five words and to give us only those chunks which are notably more frequent than in writing (**key** chunks), we still find a predominance of chunks that refer to the state of play between the speaker and listener, with *do you know what I mean* and *I know what you mean* in the top ten of the list, each occurring hundreds of times.

But what does all that mean for a model of grammar that likes to chop things up into SVOCA elements? One explanation is that verbs such as *know, think, see* and *mean* have become grammaticalized. **Grammaticalization** refers to how words from the conventional word classes (nouns, verbs, adjectives, etc.) evolve to become used differently. For example, *I'm going to sell this car* (meaning a future plan) has 'grammaticalized' the original expression *be going to* in *I'm going to New York*, so that it means something new and different (Bybee 2010: ch. 6). Rather than as S and V elements that are typically used transitively, *you know, I think*, etc. have grammaticalized to function most frequently as pragmatic markers (for further examples, see McCarthy 2021: ch. 6).

WE'RE BEGINNING TO SEE A PATTERN HERE

Another thing that corpora in general have shown us is that there are distinct patterns formed by lexical words and grammatical constructions working together. Pure formal, structural grammars see the elements in a clause (subject, verb, object, etc.) as 'slots' to be filled. *John cooked/sliced/ate the cake* all conform to the same structure, with the verb 'slot' filled by numerous different items which make grammatical sense.

Consider the verb *want*. In the Spoken BNC2014, I find 72 examples of the following construction by keying in a string of commands combining open [in square brackets] and closed (underlined) 'slots':

> pronoun *I* + [negative auxiliary/modal] + [verb in the base form] + pronoun *you* + [verb in *to*-infinitive form]

An utterance such as *I don't need you to attend* would fit that pattern, and we could dream up other verbs to fill the verb slots (*can't expect you to attend / wouldn't want you to attend*). However, when we look at the 72 examples, what we find seems to be constrained by what the main verb is. The verb *want* accounts for 59 of the examples (81 per cent). The other 13 main verb occurrences are *convince* (1 example), *get* (1), *trust* (2), *allow* (1), *need* (5), *expect* (3). Table 6.1 shows what occurs in the auxiliary/modal space.

Want appears to be a frequent verb, but it is overwhelmingly preceded by *don't*, and the only modal verb we find before it is *wouldn't*. It does not seem to occur with *can't* or *couldn't*. In this data, the auxiliary/modal 'slot' is not a free-for-all but is quite constrained. It seems the lexis and grammar are working together, not separately, to create a preference for a non-hedged pattern with the negative of *I want*.

Table 6.1 Auxiliary and modal patterns

Auxiliary or modal	Main verb	No. of occurrences
don't	want	51
didn't	want	4
wouldn't	want	2
would not	want	1
don't	need	5
wouldn't	expect	3
can't	convince	1
couldn't	get	1
can't	trust	1
don't	trust	1
didn't	expect	1
won't	allow	1

Because we can observe hundreds of patterns of this kind, it is often more useful to think of grammar and lexis as being two parts of the same harmonious system of meaning-making, or *lexicogrammar*, as Michael Halliday put it (Halliday 1996: 4). This approach to grammar was one that John Sinclair at the University of Birmingham, UK, adopted in his corpus research projects. Sinclair showed how forms and meanings were interrelated: Repeated meanings resulted in repeated forms, and the form-meaning fusions *are* the grammar. Two other Birmingham linguists, Susan Hunston and Gill Francis, applied these principles in what they called **pattern grammar** (Hunston and Francis 2000).

For Sinclair, unlike for Chomsky, what matters is not what is *possible* in grammar, but what actually *happens* (Sinclair 1991). This doesn't contradict Hopper's emergent view of grammar, nor Halliday's view of grammar as systematic. For Halliday too, the most important data were 'observed language events' (Halliday 1961: 243), but he also accepted the need for a usable description of the grammar as a system. It is not enough just to have a corpus and lots of statistics pulled out of it:

[T]he corpus does not write the grammar for us. Descriptive categories do not emerge out of the data. Description is a theoretical activity; and ... a theory is a designed semiotic system, designed so that we can explain the processes being observed.

(Halliday 1996: 24)

'I SEE HIM YESTERDAY': DIALECT GRAMMARS

Here are some examples of grammar you hear regularly in the place where I write this book, a village in the east of England in the county of Cambridgeshire. Standard English versions are given on the right.

I see him yesterday.	I saw him yesterday.
That rained last night.	It rained last night.
We was too late.	We were too late.
I went to her house but she weren't there.	... she wasn't there.
I ain't paying £20 for that!	I'm not paying £20 for that!
A: It's a big tractor. B: That it is!	A: It's a big tractor. B: It is!

None of the forms on the left are wrong; they are simply different from the forms of the British educated standard. The educated standard, the model taught in schools, is generally not associated with any one part of the country; that is why it is called a 'standard'. Versions of grammar associated with particular regions of countries are **dialect grammars**.

I live in eastern England, but I was born and raised in south Wales. I grew up with some features of non-standard grammar which were normal for me in the first 20 years of my life (standard versions on the right):

I loves ice-cream.	I love ice-cream.
He works in Newport, and she do.	He works in Newport, and she does.
He don't live here no more.	He doesn't live here anymore.
Let's go home, is it?	Let's go home, shall we?

She've eaten all that pie.	She has eaten all that pie.
There's lovely!	That's lovely!
I seen her the other say.	I saw her the other day.
They didn't have cars in them days.	They didn't have cars in those days.

In the dialect of my place of birth, present tense regular verbs can take an -*s* ending for all persons (*I likes, you likes, he/she likes, we likes, they likes*). The negative auxiliary verb *doesn't* is a rarity; *don't* can be used for all persons (*I don't like it, he/she don't like it*), and the final -*t* of *don't* is rarely pronounced. Auxiliary *have* can be used for all persons (e.g. *he/she've gone away*). *There's* can be followed by an adjective (*there's lovely/daft/awful*). The use of *them* as a demonstrative determiner instead of *those* is found in many dialects in Britain and Ireland and also in the United States (Hazen et al. 2011). Dialect grammatical forms are often shared in geographically separated areas (Milroy and Milroy 1999: 69–73). As an English speaker from Cardiff, South Wales, I felt quite at home when I discovered this wonderful bench in Northern Ireland:

Figure 6.1 'Sometimes I just sits.'
Source: Image © Michael McCarthy 2019.

In the Cambridgeshire examples listed earlier, *that* is often used where the standard uses pronoun *it* (*that rained, that's two o'clock*), and parts of the past tense of the verb *to be* are more or less in reverse of standard English, as if they were swapped around:

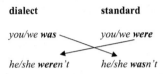

dialect	standard
*you/we **was***	*you/we **were***
*he/she **weren't***	*he/she **wasn't***

In fact, it is often the most basic verbs (*be, do, have*) which vary in their forms around the dialects of Britain and Ireland. We also see variation in how the past is referred to. In my Cambridgeshire village, *I see him yesterday* uses the standard present-tense form instead of standard *saw*; other dialects use the standard past participle *seen* (*I seen him yesterday*). In some dialects, the past tense form (*wrote, took, spoke*) is used where standard English would use the past participle (*written, taken, spoken*). Here are some remarks I have noted down:

I haven't wrote my article yet. (remark by an American academic)
It's raining now and she haven't took her umbrella. (South Wales)
I ain't spoke to him about it yet. (Cambridgeshire)

The dog-owner in my village in Cambridgeshire who looked at his dog begging and said *that boy want a biscuit* was using a dialect form (no -*s* ending on third-person present tense verbs) which is found in the neighbouring county of Norfolk too (Trudgill 2016). Dialect forms spread as people move around and contact one another.

The grammar-checker on my computer has almost exploded trying to correct all the dialect examples I have given so far in this chapter!

Welsh dialects of English are well-documented (e.g. Penhallurick 2007), and I am still happy to use some of the South Welsh forms when I visit my place of birth and meet up with family and old friends. I am more reluctant to use the bits of grammar listed for my present home county of Cambridgeshire, where I have lived for more than 30 years, though the forms are infectiously appealing, and I do catch myself out using them now and then.

My willingness or reluctance to use dialect forms is because our dialect is part of our identity; it is a badge of belonging. I feel I belong to the South Welsh community I grew up in. In the village where I currently live, after 33 years I am no longer considered a 'blow-in', but I always feel a little hesitant as regards claiming full membership of the linguistic community.

To attempt to supress dialects, as tyrants have done over the course of history, is to deny people's sense of identity and community, and to insist that children learn the standard in school to the exclusion of their dialect is equally wrong. Some of the older residents of my village recall being chastised by schoolteachers for using dialect forms. In an ideal world, we respect the rights of children to use their dialect at the same time as teaching them the social usefulness of the standard in the situations where it is most appropriate. But we should not shy away from discussion of the way class snobbishness and prejudice often lead to dialect speakers being looked down upon or judged as less intelligent.

ENGLISH GRAMMAR AROUND THE WORLD

British English in various dialect forms had a huge influence historically on the development of national varieties of English around the world. England colonised Ireland and Scotland in Mediaeval times, and over the centuries the Gaelic languages were pushed into ever-smaller corners of the island of Ireland and of Scotland as English took over. But it was not all one-way and the English of Scotland and Ireland had a strong influence on the development of English in North America because of emigration. And now American English is influencing British English.

Ireland retains its distinctive national variety of English. For example, Irish English has a way of using a construction with *be* + *after* +*-ing* to refer to the past. The Irish English speaker who says *I've chocolate around somewhere and I'm after forgetting where I put it* would probably say *I've chocolate around somewhere and I've forgotten where I put it* if they were to use standard British English grammar.

The Irish linguist Anne O'Keeffe and the Spanish linguist Carolina Amador Moreno, both of whom specialise in corpus studies of Irish English, looked at corpus evidence for the use of the *be* + *after* +*-ing* construction. The construction can be traced to influence from the Gaelic Irish language and has been used as a stereotype of 'stage Irish' speech, which is often looked upon as inferior to British English. However, O'Keeffe and Amador Moreno's analysis shows that it has developed some specialised functions in Irish English that have no obvious equivalents in standard English, which explains why it has survived as a distinctive dialect feature. The functions of *be + after +-ing* include an emphasis on the immediacy of an event and a foregrounding function in storytelling (O'Keeffe and Amador Moreno 2009; see also Harris 1993; Hickey 2007; Corrigan 2011). The conclusion we can take from such a study is that dialect grammars are not just variants of the standard but have their own systems of meanings in their cultural contexts.

CORPUS EVIDENCE

The one-million-word Limerick Corpus of spoken Irish English (LCIE) shows examples of the construction *be + after + ing* which, in standard British English would be in the present perfect or past perfect form or the simple past. Table 6.2 shows a random sample of ten concordance lines.

Table 6.2 Concordance lines for *be + after + ing* (LCIE)

He was already	after	meeting Paudie on Friday and
Nuala goes 'I think I'm	after	insulting your mother and now I
around somewhere and I'm	after	forgetting where I put it. Just
because am because am I'm	after	going too far. They couldn't
He's gifted like. I'm	after	watching it about nine times and
something Lyons? Lyons is	after	getting a new car. Laughs Oh my
ally nice. We were just	after	getting out of the car; we were
don't know why but she's	after	telling me ten times where she
brought a seat. Are they	after	getting the disease like, take
bowl of salad and she was	after	frying rashers one morning you

The island of Ireland is also home to a very practical item of grammar that seems to be missing in standard British English grammar – a plural form of *you*, such as exists in French (*vous*), Welsh (*chi*) or Swedish (*ni*). English just has *you*, for singular or plural. Irish English has *ye* and (in the north) *yous* for the plural. *Yous(e)* is common in Australia and New Zealand English too. American and Caribbean dialects often have *y'all* with a similar meaning. In this respect, British English grammar is somewhat lacking.

These facts are important because we must never think that varieties of English are the inferior offspring of the old, respectable motherland. The corpus linguists Claudia Lange and Sven Leuckert note how Indian English was looked down upon during the colonial period. As colonial varieties of English emerged, they were 'at best treated with curiosity, at worst with imperial condescension' (Lange and Leuckert 2020: 115).

Countries where English was the colonial language and where it evolved into a distinctive local variety included areas of 'high contact' with other languages, for example, the indigenous languages of India, or Chinese languages and Malay in Malaysia and Singapore. In these situations of high contact, we often find ellipsis of pronouns like the examples of situational ellipsis discussed earlier in this chapter.

When I lived in Malaysia, I was constantly surprised by the effectiveness of communication in English by ordinary, non-professional folk who used English with aplomb in their public life even though it was not their native tongue, while I struggled to use the national language Bahasa Malaysia. I lost count of the times that small shopkeepers, unwilling to lose a potential customer, if they didn't have an item in stock, would say *don't have but can get*, whereupon a youngster would be dispatched to run or cycle to find the desired item somewhere or other while I waited over a friendly cup of tea. Simplification of standard British English grammar through ellipsis of pronouns has been observed in corpus data of Indian English and Singapore English too (Tamaredo 2018). *Simplification* is a charged word; it should not be equated with 'simplistic' or simplicity of thinking. It is a highly economical and efficient process that makes communication work with minimal effort and resources for all parties involved, speakers and listeners.

LISTEN UP AND CHECK THIS OUT!

American English (AmE) is a variety covering not only the many dialects of the North American continent but is also one that occupies a uniquely dominant position in the world through films, pop culture, the global reach of broadcast media, social media and the learning of English as a second or foreign language. Apart from the more obvious differences of accent, vocabulary and pronunciation, some AmE grammatical features have influenced British English (BrE) in recent years. In the last 20 years, I have been involved as a text book writer with modelling American English for learners of English as a second or foreign language, and I have made observations in the form of field-notes of American grammar that I now hear more frequently in BrE than I did a decade or so ago. For instance, *likely* in BrE was normally treated as an adjective and occurred mostly in constructions such as *X is likely to happen*, which could be compared with *X is certain/sure/unlikely to happen*. AmE uses *likely* more frequently as an adverb, as in these extracts from the written section of the Open American National Corpus (OANC):

*Those questions will be **likely** answered more directly in the future …*
OANC 5963
*We **likely** misclassified some patients as moderate risk when they may have actually been high risk … OANC5638*

Although the frequency of the AmE construction in the OANC is more than 15 times greater than in the BNC1994, the AmE construction is increasingly heard in BrE, especially among journalists and media commentators. Another construction that has found its way into BrE and other varieties of English from AmE is the use of *be like* to report speech (*I was like 'No way!'*), which the linguists Sali Tagliamonte and Rachel Hudson see as an example of global diffusion of what was a feature of AmE usage (Tagliamonte and Hudson 1999); we will return to *like* in Chapter 8. Yet another one is to say *me either*, which, in my standard BrE grammar would be *nor me*.

We might also note the AmE preference for turning single lexical verbs into phrasal verbs, so that we *check things out, we listen up, we wait up*, as well as a love of phrasal verbs in general that you can find anywhere on social media: We *call out* people whose actions or ideas we find abhorrent (challenge/expose), we *double down on* our efforts to achieve something, we *push back against* things we don't want to accept or *push back* (postpone) events that are too soon, etc. The influence of AmE on BrE is one of those areas that raise people's hackles, with many seeing AmE as a negative influence on BrE, as the American linguist Lynne Murphy, who lives and works in the UK, has written so humorously about (Murphy 2018).

CONCLUSION

Spoken English consists of a multitude of dialects, varieties and different ways of using grammar. No one dialect or variety is superior, and no one feature of grammar is better or more logical. We have also seen how everyday speaking involves using common words and expressions in ways that do not easily fit into the basic sentence grammar we outlined in Chapters 2, 3 and 4 and that we need at times to rethink our terminology and rethink how grammar comes about. When we speak in real time, we don't follow grammatical rules written on tablets of stone; we all subtly shift the conventions every time we use our language. Hundreds and thousands of occasions of uses gel into what we observe as chunks and patterns in data, which corpora help us to observe more objectively.

However, we also concluded that it was useful to have a systematic description of how this complex apparatus and phenomena all fit together to create meanings we can exchange with one another. But what should we teach our children? And who are the grammatical authorities? Do we need grammar police to make sure we all behave properly? These are question we take up in the next chapter.

FURTHER READING

Leech, G. 2000. Grammars of spoken English: New outcomes of corpus-oriented research. *Language Learning* 50 (4): 675–724.
This is a survey of all the arguments about spoken versus written grammars in the corpus linguistics context. Geoffrey Leech argues for a unified view that respects

the differences while promoting the importance of what spoken and written grammars share.

Carter, R. and McCarthy, M. J. 1997. *Exploring Spoken English*. Cambridge: Cambridge University Press.
In this book, Ronald Carter and I present a selection of transcripts of speaking from the CANCODE corpus of everyday spoken English, with line-by-line commentaries on points of grammar and other features of usage.

Lange, C. and Leuckert, S. 2020. *Corpus Linguistics for World Englishes*. Abingdon, Oxon: Routledge.
Lange and Leuckert take us around the world looking at varieties of English and how corpora can contribute to our understanding of the different Englishes, including the English of second and foreign language learners and English as a lingua franca.

Kirkpatrick, A. 2007. *World Englishes*. Cambridge: Cambridge University Press.
Andy Kirkpatrick's book is aimed primarily at teachers of English as a foreign language, but it is of interest to anyone who wants to learn about different varieties of English. It explores English in parts of the world where it is spoken as a main or important language, as well as English as a lingua franca.

7

GRAMMAR POLICY, GRAMMAR POLITICS AND GRAMMAR POLICE

MORAL PANIC

In this chapter we look at how grammar has been in and out of fashion in school curriculums in several countries of the English-speaking world and controversies that have surrounded the teaching of English grammar. At present, grammar is firmly embedded in the National Curriculum of England and forms part of children's education from age six onwards. By the time they leave primary school, children are expected to have a grasp of sophisticated grammatical concepts such as subordination, adverbials, noun phrases and continuous verb aspect. Of course, good teaching and well-designed materials can put complex ideas over without constantly using jargon and in an enjoyable way, as good teachers and good teaching materials have always managed to do.

However, there is a lingering feeling among some people, including politicians, that the nation's grammar is not in a healthy state and that this reflects something about general social standards. Grammar is sometimes presented as evidence of the decline of the moral fabric of society and causes **moral panics**. Moral panics happen when people feel that something is threatening moral standards in society. This could be anything from social media, the lyrics of rap music, violence on TV, long hair on men, muggings, fake news, gang warfare, sexual behaviour, or declining standards of grammar and grammar teaching. All of these have been the cause of moral panics over the last 50–60 years.

Moral panics 'appeal to people who are alarmed by an apparent fragmentation or breakdown of the social order, which leaves them at risk in some way' (Thompson 1998: 3). There are people who see grammar as a reflection of social order, manners and good conduct. Any change to the 'rules' or conventions may threaten that feeling of ordered conduct in society – and that could be dangerous.

Moral panics with regard to grammar have often taken the form of media feeding frenzies around some point or other of grammatical correctness, as we shall see in Chapter 8. When judged as instances of 'bad grammar', these points of contention are seen as evidence of moral decline, particularly in groups of users who are associated with 'bad' usage (typically youngsters, users of social media, and so on): 'in the public consciousness, attitudes to standard English and "correct" use of grammar can be linked to "good" and "bad" language: good and bad people' (Jones 2017).

Grammatical moral panics range from arguments over the correct/incorrect usage of individual words to wider, general disquiet over the state of a nation's grammar. It is easy to find online debates over matters of agreement of number (e.g. *less cars* versus *fewer cars*), subject–verb concord, use or non-use of the apostrophe, worries about details of punctuation and a variety of other preoccupations. We return to some of these in Chapter 8.

When it comes to debates over the decline of general grammatical standards, public and official opinion can be merciless, satirised in this quote from Ronald Carter, a linguist who himself was the target of media criticism in the 1990s for his views on the role of English language teaching in the UK National Curriculum (see later in this chapter). Here he is commenting on the way public authorities view perceived threats to grammatical standards: 'There is a clear connection made in such thinking between grammatical order and the social order where it is only a small step from splitting infinitives to splitting heads open on football terraces' (Carter 1997: 21).

Moral panics about individual grammatical points, which we show examples of in Chapter 8, come and go. But general feelings of unease about grammatical standards are longer lasting and have been with us for centuries.

One persistent cause of public unease is the claim that a generation of adults in English-speaking countries now in their forties, fifties and sixties were let down by school systems that neglected grammar and turned them out into a world where they struggled with literacy and self-expression. This particular moral panic came to a head in the 1980s and 1990s and has not gone away, despite reforms to school curriculums in the 1990s and 2000s which brought grammar back into the classroom. Some feel that the neglect of the generation of the 1960s, 1970s and 1980s has not been properly rectified in the generations that followed. This underlying unease occasionally bubbles to the surface and the moral panic alarm bells ring in the press and broadcast media.

THE LOST GENERATION

GRAMMAR IN THE LOCKDOWN

In 2020, the year that marked the onset of the Coronavirus global pandemic, parents and guardians all over the world suddenly found themselves cast in the role of home-school teachers as schools closed down. Three sets of parents who are personal acquaintances of mine and who know my profession have spoken to me of the difficulty of teaching English grammar at home to their children. They complain that they were never taught any grammar at school and now feel hopelessly out of their depth. It is not at all uncommon to hear people in their forties and fifties confessing their ignorance of grammar.

During the UK national lockdown of April–July 2020, newspapers, broadcasting organisations and social media platforms sprang to the rescue and offered parents and guardians home-schooling advice and materials they could use with their children. The *Sunday Times* newspaper had a special section called *Home Classroom*, with the subtitle *Funday Times* designed to support home schooling and, as we can see, it was meant to be fun. School subjects including maths, science and English were presented with colourful images and diagrams. There were English grammar exercises. Here is one of them, aimed at Year 3 children (8 to 9 years old):

3 Which conjunction would not make sense in this sentence?
One of his most fascinating powers is the ability to travel back in time _____ he can collect precious historic artefacts never seen by modern humans.

a) because   c) if

b) so   d) since

(*The Sunday Times, Home Classroom* section 10 May 2020: 6)

The odd one out is **c)**. This is not too difficult for an adult whose first language is English; the word *if* would sound just wrong here. But explaining how the answer is arrived at to an inquisitive child could be hard, especially if you were trying to explain the difference between *because, so* and *since*.

Occasionally, the newspaper made life a little more difficult, as in an exercise for the same age group (8–9 years) where the task was to identify and underline subordinate clauses in example sentences. The sentences were built around a fantasy conversation between a child and a box of crayons. One of them was: 'Because of this, I need to ask you to give me some time off from colouring' (*The Sunday Times, Home Classroom* section 7 June 2020: 6).

The correct answer was to underline *because of this*. If you have read Chapter 2 of this book, you will know that *because of this* is a phrase, not a clause, since it has no verb.

Being a know-all academic and feeling a tad pedantic, I got on my high horse and complained to the newspaper about this confusing exercise. I received a sympathetic and illuminating reply from the Supplements Editor. She was not personally responsible for writing the exercise, but she acknowledged that the published exercises needed to be understood by non-teacher parents as well as by the children themselves. She generously apologised for the mistake and added that she and a colleague with whom she had discussed it had agreed they had never learnt anything as complex as subordinate clauses in primary school. The editor was not alone. Many adults will tell you they never learnt about subordinate clauses at any point in their education, nor about anything to do with grammar, for that matter.

The lockdown and home schooling brought to light a problem that had been there for a long time: Generations of people had gone through education without being taught grammar. It is no wonder that they find it difficult to help the children in their care to navigate their way through the current demands of the National Curriculum for English.

One of the reasons why there are generations of adults who never studied grammar is that there was a movement in a number of countries to abandon traditional grammar teaching as being too abstract, too difficult and not much use to anyone. But what exactly was this 'traditional' grammar that people wanted to get rid of?

WHAT DID TRADITIONAL GRAMMAR LOOK LIKE?

The most traditional sort of English grammar teaching was Latin-based, and it depended heavily on exercises in sentence **parsing**, breaking sentences into their parts and labelling them. This model dominated the teaching of English grammar for centuries well into the twentieth century. Terminology was borrowed from the terms used to describe Latin grammar, and then applied to English. The models for correctness were usually the works of great English literary writers.

Figure 7.1 shows a page from a typical little English grammar primer for young children that was used in England at the end of

FOR BEGINNERS.   33

RECAPITULATORY EXERCISE (XXII).

☞ Parse the sentences in Exercises xii., xv., xvi., xvii., xviii., xix., xx., and xxi., in the following way :—

Sentence.—*That little boy in the field held his mamma's hand.*

That   ... Pronoun. Demonstrative Adjective.
Little ... Adjective. Positive Degree.
Boy ...... Noun. Common. Masculine Gender. Singular Number. Third Person. Nominative Case ; because it comes before the Verb *held*, and answers a question beginning with *who*. (27.)
In......... Preposition.
The ...... Article.
Field   ... Noun. Common. Neuter. Singular Number. Third Person.
Held   ... Verb.＊
His ...... Pronoun. Possessive Adjective.
Mamma's Noun. Common. Feminine Gender. Singular Number. Third Person. Possessive Case; because it shews possession, and answers a question beginning with *whose*. (29.)
Hand ...... Noun. Common. Neuter. Singular Number. Third Person. Objective Case ; because it comes after the Verb *held*, and answers a question beginning with *what*. (28.)

＊ Particulars of the Verb should be deferred.

Figure 7.1 Parsing.
Source: Page from *Grammar for Beginners. An Introduction to Allen and Cornwell's English School Grammar*. London: Simpkin, Marshall & Co. 1887.

the nineteenth century. This sort of exercise would have been familiar to anyone taught grammar in a British grammar school right up to the 1960s.

The exercise teaches terms which are quite complex for children to grasp such as *nominative case* and *common* and *neuter* for nouns. Latin had cases, which were shown by word-endings. These indicated whether a word was nominative (subject), accusative (object), genitive (e.g. possessive in English), dative (e.g. indirect object in English) and so on. English does not have these Latin endings; it relies on word order to indicate functions such as subject and object, as we saw in Chapter 2. It is not surprising, therefore, that many children found this kind of grammar very abstract and difficult, and also not surprising that many educational experts started seriously to question its usefulness and whether it really helped children to read, write and express themselves better.

POLICING THE GRAMMAR: TERMINOLOGY

It was not just the teaching of English which was very formal and abstract: Students learning foreign languages were also treated to the same methods. Students doing several languages had a number of different grammars to struggle with.

In response to this mix of different languages on the school syllabus, at the end of the first decade of the twentieth century, a group of academics and school educators got together to agree on a shared language so that professionals involved in describing and teaching grammar in a variety of languages might all speak with one voice. In 1911, an influential document was published in London. It had the title 'On the Terminology of Grammar'. The idea was that English secondary school students learning ancient languages (Latin and Greek) and modern foreign languages (mainly German and French), as well as English, should work with one common set of grammar terminology regardless of which language they were studying: 'Unnecessary perplexities and difficulties at present confront pupils studying several different languages at the same time, and the teacher of one language frequently undoes the work accomplished by the teacher of another' (Anonymous 1911: 4). The introduction to the report claims that a similar desire for a shared terminology existed in America at the time too.

The terminology that was published had to suit a range of languages whose grammars were quite different, and the list of published terms contains some grammatical labels that are difficult to remember, such as *retained accusative* for passive voice sentences such as *He was awarded the prize* (which we looked at in Chapter 2). Having said that, most of the terminology is the same as the terminology used in this book, so we can see what a long-lasting influence the 1911 Report had.

Although it did its best to provide terms that were useful for each of the different languages covered, the influence of Latin-based grammar was strong, as we can see in this entry in the Report which defends using the term *case* to talk about different grammatical meanings, even though English nouns do not have the case endings that Latin had. This left an inheritance of terminology which I experienced in learning the grammar of English, French, Welsh, Spanish and Latin at secondary school in the early 1960s:

> **XXXV.** That the terms 'Objective,' 'Possessive' and 'Nominative of Address' as names of Cases in English be discarded, and that so far as possible the Latin names of the Cases be used.
> Thus:-
> Instead of 'Subjective' the term *Nominative* should be used;
> Instead of 'Nominative of Address' the term *Vocative* should be used;
> Instead of 'Objective' the two terms *Accusative* and *Dative* should be used;
> Instead of 'Possessive' the term *Genitive* should be used.
> Examples
> I am; thou art; he is; etc. (Nominative)
> Where art thou, beam of light? (Vocative)
> Good day, Sir. (Vocative)
> Nobody saw me. (Accusative)
> Who saw him die? (Accusative)
> I saw Mark Antony offer him a crown. (Dative)
> Caesar's trophies.
> Caesar's images.   (Genitive)
> Caesar's murderer.
> A stone's throw.

> (Anonymous 1911: 25)

The terminology recommended in the 1911 Report became the standard language for talking about grammar for many decades. A popular English grammar of the 1940s tells the reader that it is based on the Report (Allen and Mason 1939), and many of the terms recommended survive to this day. The 1911 Report represented the first major attempt to police the way scholars and teachers talked about grammar and it is important to understand the role it had in bolstering the teaching of what we call traditional grammar.

As the twentieth century dawned, Latin-based grammar was still dominant, and laboriously listing all the persons and tenses of verbs was considered a necessary exercise. One influential grammarian, J. C. Nesfield, who wrote several popular grammars, also gave emphasis to the construction of sentences and advice on good writing and composition in his 1898 *Manual of English Grammar and Composition* (see my discussion of it in McCarthy 2021). Nesfield also wrote grammar primers for schools. In the 1920s, his *Outline of English Grammar* (Nesfield 1920) tasked school pupils with converting compound sentences to complex ones:

> **136. From Compound to Complex.** —In a Compound sentence the second of two co-ordinate clauses is the one that completes the sense, and is therefore the more important of the two.
>
> Hence it follows that in transforming a Compound sentence to a Complex one, the *second* must be made the *Principal* or *Containing* clause, and the *first* the *Dependent* or *Contained* clause.
>
> *Compound.* Speak the truth, *and* you need have no fear.
> *Complex. If* you speak the truth, you need have no fear.
> *Compound.* Leave this room, *or* I will compel you to do so.
> *Complex. Unless* you leave this room, I will compel you to do so.
> *Compound.* He was a poor man, *but* he was always honest.
> *Complex. Although* he was poor, he was always honest.
> *Compound.* He was very tired, *and* therefore he fell sound asleep.
> *Complex.* He fell sound asleep, *because* he was very tired.
> *Exercise* 36.
> *Convert from Compound to Complex :—*
> 1.   Hand over the prisoner to me, and I will examine him.
> 2.   Take care of the pence, and the pounds will take care of themselves.

3.   Only hold your tongue, and you can hold anything else.
4.   He stands up to speak, and every one is at once silent.
5.   Is any man sick? let the elders pray for him.—*New Test.*
6.   I go to this place and that, and the same thought pursues me
everywhere.

(Nesfield 1920: 160–1)

This is different from the parsing exercise of the 1880s exercise in
Figure 7.1, but it is still very mechanical and must have been quite
challenging for some youngsters. Nesfield was a colonial official of
the British Empire in India, where his books were widely used, so
it was not just in England that this approach to grammar dominated. All over the English-speaking world, traditional grammar
was the norm.

The grammar in Figure 7.1 and the 1911 recommended terminology of cases look antiquated now, but Ronald Carter, the UK
applied linguist who worked extensively on grammar for schools in
the 1990s, showed that mechanical exercises in identifying parts of
speech were still around in the early 1960s in English school
examinations for 16 year-olds (Carter 1997: 19–20).

People sometimes talk about reviving 'traditional grammar
teaching' when they feel present-day standards are lapsing, but it is
important to understand what school pupils were exposed to in the
era of traditional grammar teaching. If we advocate a return to
traditional grammar, we should be careful what we wish for.

In the next sections, we look at how this type of formal grammar was rejected in different parts of the English-speaking world
during the second half of the twentieth century before making a
comeback in a different form at the end of the century.

(DIS-)UNITED STATES

Grammar teaching fell out of favour in the United States in the
second half of the twentieth century. As long as a hundred years
ago, voices were heard condemning Latin-based traditional grammar teaching as not helping to make the nation's children literate.
But the movements in grammar which we discussed in Chapter 5
had an even bigger influence on the decline of traditional grammar
teaching. The structuralism of grammarians such as Charles C. Fries

and the transformational-generative grammar of Noam Chomsky, each in a different way, made it more difficult to defend the teaching of traditional, Latin-based grammar.

The problem in the United States was that teachers faced with grammar based on Chomsky's theories found the teaching materials very difficult to use. As two American scholars put it with regard to the kinds of tree-diagrams we saw in Chapter 5: 'Teachers were ill-prepared for grammatical explanations that looked more like mathematics than grammar. The rejection of transformational grammar spelled the rejection of the other "new grammar" as well' (Kolln and Hancock 2005: 15).

The other 'new grammar' they are referring to here is structuralism, which was also seen as too radical and different, even though it was dedicated to describing English on its own terms and not via Latin. It was easier either to continue to teach traditional, Latin-based grammar, with all its faults, or to absorb grammar into the teaching of reading and writing and to take a more 'whole language' approach. This was a top-down view which, at its simplest, followed the principle that teaching reading and writing and letting children develop as whole persons would enable grammar to take care of itself.

Some experts saw grammar teaching as having a positively harmful effect on children's development, which Kolln and Hancock summed up as leading to 'the anti-grammar policy that has dominated the American English curriculum for forty years' (2005: 16). This trend was particularly noticeable in the 1980s. There was also an anti-elitist element involved, with more respect being paid to pupils' non-standard home-language dialects and the downplaying of formal, 'correct', rule-based grammar. The abandonment of formal grammar was, in all respects, based on the best of intentions.

AUSTRALIA: WHOLE LANGUAGE OR BITS AND PIECES?

The 'whole language' debate was played out in Australia too, and it has been blamed for creating a moral panic there (Gannon and Sawyer 2007). Writing in 1999, an Australian scholar, Nan Bernard, noted that grammar had not featured prominently in the English curriculums of Australian states for almost three decades

(Bernard 1999). As in the United States, the abandonment of grammar was put down to the belief that grammar teaching did not help schoolchildren achieve literacy.

Bernard also remarked that, although attempts were made to raise the profile of grammar teaching in the 1990s, teachers were ill-trained to deliver English grammar lessons, since nether their degree studies (typically in English literature) nor their teacher training involved any systematic study of the language. If you are in such a position, you may lack confidence in your ability to understand the subject, let alone teach it. Michael Halliday, whose grammar we looked at in Chapter 5, had grasped this in the 1960s. His grammar depends on understanding texts in their social contexts, rather than simply following a set of rules. He worked extensively in the UK and in Australia in the educational context and he recognised the difficulties teachers untrained in language study might face:

> [T]eaching the English language is a highly specialized task, perhaps the most important one in the school, and [that] only the professionally trained English language teacher can perform it. If it is left in the hands of amateurs – and the English literature specialist who has no linguistic training is almost as much an amateur in this context as is the scientist or mathematician – we can expect the result to be a nation of inarticulates, just as a nation of innumerates would result if mathematics teachers were not trained in mathematics.
>
> (Halliday 1967/2007: 26)

In Australia, as in the United States, traditional grammar teaching became absorbed into the teaching of writing and composition, and a top-down, whole language approach became dominant, even though Bernard (1999) shows that progressive ideas about grammar which rejected old Latin-based models were enshrined in official documents. A generation of teachers untrained in grammar teaching understandably failed to engage with new ideas, however appealing.

THE UK: FROM GRAMMAR TO COMPREHENSIVE

Although the education systems are different in the United States, Australia and the UK, the trends in the twentieth century with regard to grammar teaching were similar. Until the mid-1960s, secondary schools in Britain were of two main types: Grammar schools and secondary modern schools. To get into a grammar school, you took an examination at 11 years old, and the education in grammar school was strict, academic and based on formal ways that dated back centuries. I should know. I went to one. Teachers wore academic gowns and our English teacher taught us how to take sentences to pieces (parsing). We learnt about subjects, predicates, objects, adverbials and so on. We also studied Latin, where we learnt about nominatives, accusatives and ablative absolutes. All the paraphernalia of Latin grammar got mixed up with English grammar and some of it spilled over into ways of talking about English (e.g. analysing *datives* and *gerunds*).

One positive by-product of learning English grammar in this way was that it helped to make learning the grammar of the other languages on our school syllabus (Welsh, French and Spanish) more accessible, since those other languages had things like accusative (object) and dative (indirect object) pronouns and subjunctive moods. That did not necessarily make life any easier, but it did suggest there might be some good reason for learning all these abstract, rule-based systems. I personally loved traditional grammar, or I would probably not be writing this book today, but many of my peers struggled with it and could see no benefit in learning English grammar, let alone Latin or Welsh grammar.

The British secondary modern schools of the time were more angled towards the everyday needs of the economy, with most pupils ending up in manual or more menial types of jobs. Grammar schools had more middle-class pupils; secondary modern schools were dominated by working-class children.

It was understandable that people reacted against such an unequal system, and in the late 1960s and 1970s, Britain moved towards comprehensive education and non-selective schools. And in the same way, and for the same reasons that we have discussed in relation to the United States and Australia, grammar teaching declined in popularity.

Two linguists, Richard Hudson and John Walmsley, pointed out that the teaching of English in UK primary and secondary schools was dominated in the 1960s by the teaching of literature and creativity in writing and that: 'Grammar was mere mechanics, which children could be taught as and when it was relevant, or which they could just be left to pick up for themselves' (Hudson and Walmsley 2005: 609).

We have just looked at three countries, but 'the "death of grammar teaching" was a feature of most English-speaking countries at about the same time' (Hudson and Walmsley 2005: 593), So, there is every reason to believe that a number of countries ended up with 'lost generations' of people who never had a formal education in English grammar.

We can summarise the main ideas that dominated the grammar teaching debate. They all contributed in one way or another to the decline of grammar teaching in the English-speaking world in the mid- to late-twentieth century:

- Formal, rule-based grammar teaching does not promote good writing and literacy.
- Old, Latin-based models are elitist and have no place in modern, non-selective education.
- Children learn best through child-centred education.
- A 'whole language approach', where children read, write and create is more beneficial than taking the language to pieces in formal grammar teaching.
- Children's heritage languages and their dialects should be respected, and they should not be forced to adapt to the educated standard.
- New theories of grammar are all very well; putting them into practice is a different thing altogether.
- Teachers are ill-equipped by their training to teach complex models of grammar and are understandably confused by official curriculum documents.
- Many of the great grammars of the twentieth century were influential in the academic world but failed to make connections with school teaching.

A BALANCING ACT

GRAMMAR MAKES A COMEBACK

The discussion that follows is mostly about the UK, since it is the country that I have the most direct knowledge of, but the arguments apply equally to other countries in the English-speaking world. In the UK during the 1980s, the more liberal attitudes towards formal education (whole child, whole language, etc.) were subject to some re-thinking, against the background of the conservative philosophy associated with the then Prime Minister, Margaret Thatcher.

In 1988, an important document, the Kingman Report, was published by the UK government. It was prepared by a panel of experts who looked into the teaching of English language. Its opening page contained this remark:

> [T]here is a widespread concern that pressures on time and energy, together with inadequacies in the professional education and training of teachers and a misunderstanding of the nature of children's learning, are causing important areas of English language teaching to be neglected, to the detriment of children's facility with words.
>
> (The Kingman Report 1988: 1)

The report went on:

> The distraction today is in part the belief that this capacity can and should be fostered only by exposure to varieties of English language; that conscious knowledge of the structure and working of the language is unnecessary for effective use of it; that attempting to teach such knowledge induces boredom, damages creativity and may yet be unsuccessful; and that the enterprise entails imposing an authoritarian view of a standard language which will be unacceptable to many communities in our society.
>
> (ibid.)

These are familiar themes. The Kingman Report recommended that grammatical knowledge should be part of a child's education, not for its own sake as a set of abstract rules, but rather as a tool to understand how language changes over time, the various dialects and non-standard grammars of English, the syntax of complex sentences in writing, and so on.

Likewise, in Australia, moves to adopt a model based on Michael Halliday's systemic-functional grammar were a balance of knowledge about grammatical forms and conventions combined with understanding the role of grammar in society. The Australian

Curriculum for English of May 2009 made clear the link between knowledge of grammatical form and an understanding of texts, and how these relate to broader communication skills. This is the outline of the language strand for children 8–12 years old.

5.8 Years 3–6 (typically 8–12 years of age)
5.8.1 Language Strand:

Students develop an increasingly sophisticated understanding about grammar and language features and are increasingly able to articulate these understandings. More complex punctuation, clause and sentence structures, and textual purposes and patterns are introduced. This deeper understanding includes more explicit metalanguage as students learn to classify words, sentence structures, and texts. To consolidate both 'learning to read' and 'reading to learn', students explore the language features of different types of texts, including visual texts, advertising, digital/online and media texts.

(https://docs.acara.edu.au/resources/Australian_
Curriculum_-_English.pdf)

In the United States, similar debates have taken place over achieving a balance between knowledge about grammar and how it helps children to understand how language works and how people use it in society (whether in their dialects or heritage languages, or in composition and writing). A good summary of the arguments is to be found in the article by Kolln and Hancock (2005) referred to earlier. They end with a statement of their goal:

We would aim at a program embracing deep and wide knowledge of grammar as highly useful, perhaps proclaiming that ignorance of grammar is far more limiting than knowledge, that it creates a vacuum within which dysfunctional prescriptive norms are enforced. We would aim for a program that values home languages as the foundation for the evolution of a highly effective writing voice.

(Kolln and Hancock 2005: 29)

It looked as if we were about to enter a golden age of compromise in which grammatical knowledge would be on the menu again, but taken away from its abstract, Latin-based approaches to a more socially useful thread in the national or state curriculums of the three countries we have looked at.

INFORMATION ADD-ON

The UK Kingman Report was balanced in its views about the teaching of English. It rejected extreme views from both sides of the argument, as we see in this paragraph:

> Nor do we see it as part of our task to plead for a return to old-fashioned grammar teaching and learning by rote. We have been impressed by the evidence we have received that this gave an inadequate account of the English language by treating it virtually as a branch of Latin, and constructing a rigid prescriptive code rather than a dynamic description of language in use. It was also ineffective as a means of developing a command of English in all its manifestations. Equally, at the other extreme, we reject the belief that any notion of correct or incorrect use of language is an affront to personal liberty. We also reject the belief that knowing how to use terminology in which to speak of language is undesirable.
>
> (The Kingman Report 1988: 3)

For more on the Kingman Report and the debates that surrounded it, see Milroy and Milroy (1999: ch. 8).

FROM BALANCE TO MORAL PANIC

We might assume that a healthy balance in grammar teaching between a formal description of the grammar and the study of how it is put to use in texts and in society would please everyone. In the UK, the post-1988 National Curriculum brought grammar back into the classroom in a version that encouraged the study of variation in dialects and differences between speaking and writing but, at the same time, aimed to arm school-leavers with a systematic knowledge of standard grammar. However, in the UK at least, there was still the problem of a poorly prepared teaching profession, with many younger teachers having gone through the lost years in their own education and, through no fault of their own, knowing little about grammar.

My colleague at the University of Nottingham, Ron Carter, tried to remedy the situation by creating a bank of materials for teachers called LINC (Language in the National Curriculum), the fruits of a government-funded project which was developed around 1990. That was when the trouble began.

Even though the UK government had commissioned the project, it did not at all like the materials that were produced and banned their publication. The government felt that the materials did not promote correct standard English. The materials had to go underground and were made available in various formats (see https://clie.org.uk/linc/). They proved to be popular among teachers. But the banning of the materials spelt trouble for Ron Carter who had to defend himself against hostile sections of the media and I clearly recall one media outlet at the time calling him 'Red Ron'.

Tensions in the UK continued well into the early 2000s, with grammar now firmly established as an element of the National Curriculum. Not everyone was happy with this new systematic approach to grammar. In 2005, the *Independent* newspaper had the headline: 'Schools "are wasting their time teaching grammar"' (the *Independent* 19 January 2005, https://www.independent.co.uk/news/education/education-news/schools-are-wasting-their-time-teaching-grammar-5344776.html).

Lined up were two opposing camps. One was a group of academics who claimed their research showed that formal grammar teaching had no impact on children's ability to write. The *Independent* article goes on: 'The study, which researchers claim is the largest review of existing research on grammar teaching, is likely to embarrass ministers who have put formal grammar teaching at the heart of their drive to raise literacy standards.'

Not only government ministers were potentially pitted against the educational experts. The *Independent* then went on to quote the leader of the Campaign for Real Education as saying the research results were 'absolute nonsense' and that it was 'worrying if academics are suggesting that we should go back to the laissez-faire attitudes of the 1960s'. Grammar was continuing to foment a steady moral panic that had persisted over decades.

INFORMATION ADD-ON

These are the statutory English Language elements for 7 to 8 year-olds (Year 3) in the National Curriculum for England published in 2013.

Year 3: Detail of content to be introduced (statutory requirement)

Word	Formation of nouns using a range of prefixes [for example super–, anti–, auto–] Use of the forms a or an according to whether the next word begins with a consonant or a vowel [for example, a rock, an open box] Word families based on common words, showing how words are related in form and meaning [for example, solve, solution, solver, dissolve, insoluble]
Sentence	Expressing time, place and cause using **conjunctions** [for example, *when, before, after, while, so, because*], **adverbs** [for example, *then, next, soon, therefore*], or **prepositions** [for example, *before, after, during, in, because of*]
Text	Introduction to paragraphs as a way to group related material Headings and sub-headings to aid presentation Use of the **present perfect** form of **verbs** instead of the simple past [for example, *He has gone out to play* contrasted with *He went out to play*]
Punctuation	Introduction to inverted commas to **punctuate** direct speech

(Retrieved from: https://assets.publishing.service.gov.uk/government/uploads/system/uploads/attachment_data/file/335186/PRIMARY_national_curriculum_-_English_220714.pdf)

As the English National Curriculum bedded in, creative and enjoyable methods of teaching grammar to children accompanied it. In a 2014 book aimed at primary school teachers, lesson ideas are given for putting over the grammar points. In relation to the teaching of the present perfect (see the Information add-on box above, under *Text*), the following suggestions are given:

> Use the cards from earlier (pronoun/verb/adverbial) or prepare a resource for the interactive whiteboard. Attach a selection, including regular and irregular verbs, to the board, this time adding the verb *have*. Using talk partners, give the children one minute to come up with a sentence which includes *have* next to one of the main verbs. Select pairs to say their sentences: using thumbs up/thumbs down, ask the class to indicate if they think the sentence sounds right or wrong. If thumbs go down, allow the pair to select a member of the class to explain what they think was wrong.
>
> (Horton and Bingle 2014: 70)

Later in the same book, the authors tackle the question of teaching the passive voice, with a lesson plan for children aged 10–11. The lesson is based around a text about a museum theft, with passives that include *was stolen, was arrested, was taken into custody*, which the children explore in terms of who the agents of the actions are, rather than simply what the subjects of the verbs are (Horton and Bingle 2014: 148–53).

This is a world away from parsing and the mechanical manipulation of sentences in traditional, Latin-based grammar. But the book these lessons are taken from acknowledges that many primary school teachers lack confidence in their own knowledge of grammar (since many will be members of the lost generation), so the book also takes teachers through a description of the grammar system at the same time as giving advice on teaching it.

With such a good balance of making grammatical knowledge available to teachers and finding new, enjoyable and effective ways of passing that knowledge on to children and encouraging them to use it creatively, you might assume that, finally, everyone would be happy.

MR GOVE AND MR GWYNNE

Michael Gove was UK Secretary of State for Education in 2013, a year when grammar hit the headlines again. Mr Gove had become tired of what he considered to be the poor and incorrect grammar of his civil servants. He recommended that they should use a

Figure 7.2 'He said his first fronted adverbial today.'
Source: © Jake Tebbit 2020.

book called *Gwynne's Grammar*, which is a conservative grammar primer that would not have been out of place in a 1950s grammar school.

The author, N. M. Gwynne, uses many terms that we use in this book, but he also insists on standards of correctness which go against everyday usage. For instance, when dealing with *gerunds* (the *-ing* forms of verbs acting as nouns as in *smoking is bad for you*), he insists that a possessive form must be used before them (Gwynne 2013: 39). This would apply in sentences such as:

*I look forward to **his** telling us the news in person.*

However, most people would feel quite comfortable saying:

*I look forward to **him** telling us the news in person.*

The British actor Micheal Ward, originally from Jamaica, looking back, said in an interview in the UK *Sunday Times* Magazine (22 November 2020: 33):

My dad died in a car crash. **Him** *dying was a force behind* **me** *coming to Britain.*

His and *my* instead of *him* and *me* here would sound very formal and perhaps even pompous in the context of an informal interview.

It is quite normal and acceptable to use an object pronoun (*him*) rather than the possessive determiner *his*. That is the problem when you decide on a Latin-based category and try to apply it to English: The 'logic' of abstract grammar falls down in the face of majority usage. Mr Gwynne, and presumably Mr Gove, would simply argue that the majority are wrong (and would probably insist on saying *the majority is wrong*), claiming a right to police grammatical correctness.

The UK *Daily Telegraph*'s website described Gwynne's grammar as 'dynamite to modern, child-centred education: a guide to the forgotten rudiments of the English language' (Grice 2013). In stark contrast, Oliver Kamm, writing in the *Spectator* magazine was not impressed. He called Gwynne 'an ignoramus who bungles basic grammatical concepts while insisting that certain weird peeves of his are the only "correct" way to write' (Kamm 2015).

Gwynne blamed academics and experts in child psychology in teacher training colleges for the decline in grammatical standards in an interview (Grice 2013) and was extremely prescriptive in his grammar. But he had power behind him in the form of a cabinet minister and his book became popular for a while. Mr Gove did not give up easily: In 2015 he issued a list of what he held to be grammatical 'howlers' to his staff and forbade their use (Glaze 2015). Traditional grammar was refusing to lie down.

CONCLUSION

Although the teaching of grammar in English schools was reinstated, there was still unease in public life in the second decade of the twenty-first century about grammatical standards. Moral panics about grammar and the role of schools in teaching it seem to surface periodically in the English-speaking world.

The battle between the 'top-downers' who believe in a whole-child, whole-language approach where grammar takes second place to writing and creativity, and 'bottom-uppers', where the grammatical system must first be learnt before sophisticated and creative expression become possible, will probably continue to surface from time to time. The dispute is like the opposition between the *Big-Endians* and the *Little-Endians* in Jonathan Swift's *Gulliver's Travels* (1726). The Big-Endians broke their boiled eggs at the broader end of the egg, the Little-Endians at the smaller end. The Emperor decreed that the population should break the smaller end. Wars were fought over it.

The UK has no official academy of the language or 'grammar authority'. People who are obsessed with grammatical correctness are often called 'grammar police', but mostly these are individuals who have bees in their bonnet about grammar but no power, apart from being able to vent their feelings in letters in newspapers, blogs, discussion fora and social media postings. Occasionally, politicians and others in powerful positions put their oar in and get undue levels of publicity. Power rests with the powerful in society, and their voices are often the loudest.

We have seen how the terminology of grammar that we have all inherited was handed down to us from a group of scholars and educators genuinely concerned to get some sort of uniformity into the teaching of languages. Depending on which side you take, both academics and other experts as well as politicians and journalists have too much or too little power in deciding over whether and how we teach grammar. Somewhere there must be room for dialogue and compromise, so that Big-Endians and Little-Endians listen to one another and do not fight needless grammar wars.

The Coronavirus pandemic of 2020 gave rise to new anxieties as the lost generation suddenly found that they were expected to teach grammar to their children at home as schools closed down. This chapter has exposed some of the fault lines in the education system over the years which resulted in a generation of parents and guardians ill-equipped to carry out their new, unanticipated responsibility as grammar teachers. Whether the present generation of schoolchildren who are studying grammar in the new way will find it easier to help their own children with English grammar if ever such a crisis repeats itself in the future, only time will tell.

FURTHER READING

Peterson, E. 2020. *Making Sense of 'Bad English': An Introduction to Language Attitudes and Ideologies*. Abingdon, Oxon: Routledge.
Elizabeth Peterson's book looks at the notion of standard English and the 'standard culture' that accompanies it. Education systems and standard languages can prove to be a barrier to accessing powerful cultures. Peterson shows how it is often marginalised groups of people who are demonised for 'bad' usage as changes take place in the language.

Carter, R. 1997. *Investigating English Discourse. Language, Literacy and Literature*. London: Routledge.
Chapter 3 of this book, 'The New Grammar Teaching', is particularly relevant to the discussion of the revival of grammar teaching in schools in the 1990s. Ron Carter was in favour of getting rid of traditional grammar, but he rejected the view that grammar could take care of itself. He was committed to a socially and functionally oriented grammar and the desire to give children access to knowledge about language as a means of social advancement.

Derewianka, B. M. 2012. Knowledge about language in the Australian curriculum: English. *Australian Journal of Language and Literacy* 35 (2): 127–146. Available online at: https://ro.uow.edu.au/cgi/viewcontent.cgi?article=1128&context=sspapers.
This article shows how the details of grammar are related to texts, registers and social contexts. It helps to combine in a positive way a top-down approach and a bottom-up approach. Its purpose is to offer a better understanding of the Australian Curriculum for English Language, but it can apply to any country where the school system is trying to link a whole language approach to a systematic study of grammar.

8

GRAMMAR IN THE PUBLIC EYE

THE GRAMMATICAL LANDSCAPE

Grammar is often the subject of debate and controversy in everyday, non-academic life outside of the world of schools, universities and colleges. Beyond the world of scholarly journals, reference books, school textbooks and the classroom, grammar is in the hands of its users.

Grammar is visible in the *linguistic landscape*, the language that is visible to the public eye (Landry and Bourhis 1997). We see it in signs and advertisements; we find grammar in all our daily encounters with public life, and it often becomes the subject matter of popular debate. It raises strong feelings in people, which they show in irritated social media postings and letters and emails to newspaper editors and broadcasters. Sometimes, grammar wars can be fought over just one or two small words.

LESS OR FEWER?

If you enter 'less versus fewer' into a search engine, you are likely to get millions of hits, with endless debates over correct usage and 'bad grammar' and you will encounter both easy-going and hard-line attitudes.

Traditionally, *fewer* is used with countable nouns in the plural (*fewer cars, fewer visitors, fewer birds*), while *less* is used with uncountable nouns (*less traffic, less tourism, less wildlife*). In 2008, the BBC reported that a major UK supermarket chain had decided to change the signs on quick check-outs from '10 items or less' to 'up to 10 items' after criticism in the media. In that way they avoided what might have sounded over-pedantic if they had changed the signs to '10 items or fewer'. A spokesperson for the Plain English Campaign, a group whose aim is exactly what its name suggests, was quoted in the BBC piece:

> But it can be tricky when referring to quantities, says Marie Clair from the Plain English Campaign. For example, we say less than six weeks, not fewer than six weeks, because we are not referring to six individual weeks, but to a single period of time lasting six weeks.
> 'Some people get "really roused up" about the misuse of less or fewer,' she says, 'and words that describe quantity, degree or amount seem to perplex people.'
>
> (http://news.bbc.co.uk/1/hi/magazine/7591905.stm)

'Really roused up' is quite a strong reaction to grammar, and we may think that the controversy over *less* versus *fewer* is a storm in a teacup. However, Marie Clair touches on an important issue: Grammatical choices can be determined by how we personally see the world. Six weeks can be seen as six individual things (plural) or as one period of time (singular). There is no law or logical principle to decide this choice; it is up to the individual user. In September 2020, the UK government published new restrictions on social contact as a measure to check the spread of the Covid-19 virus. One website gave guidelines concerning places of worship: 'In England, places of worship can have as many people in them as is safe to do so. Again, people can only attend in groups of six or less' (https://covid19data.com/2020/09/22/coronavirus-what-are-social-distancing-and-self-isolation-rules/).

A *group of six* is probably seen by the writer as a single unit which could be *less* in size/extent, rather than six individuals who could be reduced to *fewer* in number. These are psychological arguments rather than mathematically logical ones.

Grammar arouses strong feelings in people, and it is important to be aware of public attitudes and concerns as well as knowing what the perceived 'rules' are or how human psychology affects grammatical choices. It may well be that, for most situations, *less* will do, and *fewer* can be abandoned. However, there might be formal situations in writing where *fewer* would still sound more appropriate and less likely to offend purists and traditionalists.

CORPUS EVIDENCE

In the spoken transcripts of the BNC1994, *fewer* occurs some 6.6 times per million words. In the Spoken BNC2014, it only occurs 2.8 times per million words, so that is less than half the number of occurrences by 2014. Or should that be 'fewer than half the number of occurrences ...'?

On the other hand, the spoken Open American National Corpus, comparable in size to the two British samples, and consisting of data collected from 1990 onwards, shows an occurrence of 10 per million words for *fewer*.

This may reflect a greater grammatical conservatism in North American English, but, a note of caution: It is sometimes unwise to make comparisons between corpora in this way, since the dates and methods of data collection may vary.

PUTTING A (FULL) STOP TO PUNCTUATION

PUNCTUATION AND GRAMMAR

As we saw in Chapter 2 in relation to relative clauses, punctuation can affect the meaning of the grammar of a sentence. For many people, punctuation and grammar go hand in hand, and people are often heard to say in the same breath that they are no good at either, or else they bemoan the decline in grammatical standards and include punctuation in text messages and social media (or the lack of it).

Punctuation serves a variety of purposes, from marking sentence boundaries to signalling relationships between parts of sentences, to quoting and recreating speech, to indicating the shortening and combining of sounds, to indicating possession, to expressing emotional reactions. The linguist Paul Bruthiaux condenses these uses into two main purposes:

> One, a syntactic function, is to clarify relationships between sentences or between independent and dependent clauses. The other, a

prosodic function, is to mark some of the intonational contours that appear to many writers to accompany their texts when they read them mentally or that might surface if these texts were to be read aloud.

(Bruthiaux 1995)

FULL STOPS

The full stop (or *period* in American English) is the standard way of marking the end of a sentence in English. So, what could be simpler, more straightforward or uncontroversial than this little dot on the page? Yet the UK *Sunday Times* newspaper in 2020 published an article under the headline:

DOES IT HAVE TO END THIS WAY? THE KIDS HAVE KILLED THE FULL STOP

The article had a call-out text that began, 'Teenagers say the punctuation mark is too aggressive' (Dent 2020). The full stop, the author claims, on the evidence of online debate, is perceived by youngsters when used in social media posting and texting as implying 'sarcasm, unhappiness or even aggression' (ibid.). Who would have thought a tiny punctuation mark could upset people?

Unsurprisingly, the growth of social media and electronic communications in general have influenced punctuation. It is quick and easy to jab a short message onto the screen of a phone, press *send*, get a short response back from the other person, send them a few more words, get a few back, and so on. Such exchanges are more like the back and forth ping-pong of conversation than the carefully composed sentences of traditional writing, so it is natural that punctuation should no more play a role in these short, sharp-and-to-the-point messages than it does when we are speaking.

REFLECTION POINT

Rate your own personal use of these punctuation marks when you type emails on a computer or text messages on a phone.

Use a scale of 1–4, where 4 = *I regularly use*, 3 = *I sometimes use*, 2 = *I rarely use* and 1 = *I never use*.

Table 8.1 Emailing, texting and punctuation

	Computer emailing	*Phone texting*
. full stop/period		
, comma		
? question mark		
! exclamation mark		
; semi-colon		
: colon		
- hyphen		
' apostrophe		
' … ' quote marks		

THE RISE AND FALL OF THE SEMI-COLON

As regards your use of punctuation marks in electronic communications, I might hazard a guess that you would give the semi-colon a low score. In the text messages I've received from friends on my phone over the last few months, I cannot find a single semi-colon. On the other hand, I find commas, full stops, question marks and, everywhere, exclamation marks, sometimes two or three together!!!

Conventionally, the semi-colon is used to join two main clauses which are not linked by conjunctions, for example:

I don't like ferry crossings; I get seasick.

In this example, the two clauses could equally well be separated by a full stop or linked more explicitly by *because*, and many people would be quite happy using a comma – a practice referred to as a *comma splice*:

I don't like ferry crossings, I get seasick.

If you search the term 'comma splice' on the web, you will find lots of advice on how to *avoid* them, *fix* them, *correct* them, and you will find them referred to as *wrong*, as an *error* or as a *fault*. Strong words indeed. If you do want to 'fix' them or just avoid them, using the semi-colon is one way of doing so.

Paul Bruthiaux's 1995 article is entitled 'The Rise and Fall of the Semicolon'. He shows how, by the late eighteenth century, the semi-colon had found its place in the English punctuation system as a mark separating main clauses in sentences. Since then it seems to have fallen out of popularity, but it has not declined without a struggle amongst its supporters and detractors in punctuation manuals for popular use. Bruthiaux argues, with corpus evidence, that punctuation manuals and expert advice are out of tune with popular usage.

CORPUS EVIDENCE

If we divide the texts in the BNC 1994 into three sets, covering 1960–1974, 1975–1984 and 1985–1993, respectively, we can see a decline in the number of semi-colons.

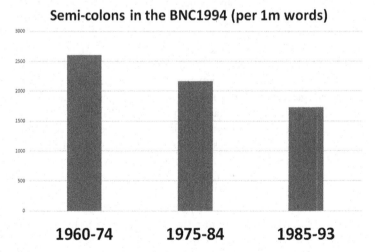

Semi-colons in the BNC1994 (per 1m words)

Figure 8.1 Semi-colons.

ENDANGERED SPECIES? THE APOSTROPHE

Recently, I attended my local clinic to get my annual flu vaccine. The friendly nurse enquired what I was a professor of. When I explained that my speciality was grammar, she said, 'Ah! The dreaded apostrophe!' – for her the first thing that sprang to mind on hearing the word *grammar*.

Moral panics about punctuation often centre around the use of the apostrophe, especially its use (or non-use) in the public domain, on street signs and similar public texts, including the so-called *greengrocer's apostrophe*, named because of a tendency for market-traders in fruit and vegetables to display hand-written signs advertising produce such as *banana's, tomato's* and *plum's*. It would be a big mistake to ignore or dismiss such moral panics; they tell us much about the things that exercise ordinary people whose lives are led outside the cosy echo-chambers of university departments and the highbrow media.

In the village that is my home, I often walk past street signs that are of different vintages. The older ones tend to include the apostrophe in the names of streets and other places which commemorate historical figures, Christian saints and erstwhile local trades such as millers, bakers and farmers. More recent ones seem to have dropped the apostrophe. Figure 8.2 shows some of these signs from my village and some from a nearby village.

Figure 8.2 shows a mixed bag of punctuation. *Millers Road* (the road once associated with the miller and which led to the local mill) has no apostrophe in one sign but does so in another, both in the same village. The name of the row of cottages dedicated to the Christian saint, Andrew, has no apostrophe. However, the *People's Hall* seems clearly to advertise itself as the property of the people, while *All Saints' Churchyard* shows itself to belong to the church of *All Saints'*, which itself boasts an apostrophe, albeit without the usual following noun. What is more, in the last few weeks, some newly built houses in another nearby village have just been given shiny new street names, including *Burdeley's Close*, proudly bearing an apostrophe. Our local authority just can't seem to make its mind up once and for all. Wherever we look, in the UK at least, we find this mixed bag of apostrophes. It is because it is so 'public' and visible in the linguistic landscape that it courts debate and controversy.

Figure 8.2 Apostrophe use in public signs.
Source: Photographs: © Michael McCarthy 2020.

The apostrophe examples presented here are from England because that is where I live, but there are plenty of examples from further afield. The American linguist Greta Little shows how writers have struggled with apostrophe use for centuries and how the inconsistent picture I've painted with images from my village has been seen around the English-speaking world:

> Canadian merchants have been more reluctant to do away with apostrophes in their business names, but they are unsure whether they want to keep them on their department labels and sale banners – Men's and Ladies Wear, Childrens section.

(Little 1986: 15)

As well as North American examples, Greta Little says of Australia: 'The suburban areas around Sydney display no apostrophes even in names such as Crows Nest, McMahons Point, and Frenchs Forest.'

There is also more recent evidence from educational contexts in New Zealand and Australia of inconsistency in apostrophe usage (Cop and Hatfield 2017).

SOUND–SPELLING GRAMMATICAL CONFUSIONS

One problem is that some common words in English which are pronounced the same or very similarly can have different meanings depending on whether they are written with an apostrophe or not. It is here that grammar and punctuation often get tangled up. Table 8.2 gives examples that I've noted in the past year, from social media postings and personal emails, of forms often confused.

Here are some non-standard examples, all anonymised except for one, which was sent out publicly by a body that should know better:

[opening to an email] *Hi Mike, I hope **your** well.*
[commenting on the gardening season] *Our apples are no good this year, we had some great **one's** last year.*
[headline in publicity email for the Cambridge Literary Festival 4 November 2020] *The World holds **it's** breath …*

Table 8.2 Word-forms often confused in writing

Standard usage			
With apostrophe	*Example*	*No apostrophe*	*Example*
one's (possessive determiner)	*do one's duty*	ones (substitute pronoun)	*I prefer the blue ones*
you're (contracted verb)	*you're late*	your (possessive determiner)	*Is this your phone?*
it's (contracted verb)	*it's easy!*	its (possessive determiner)	*the company has changed its logo*
Who's (contraction of *who is / who has*)	*Who's that tall woman over there?*	whose (possessive determiner or pronoun)	*Whose car is it?*

We should also include writing *her's, your's* and *their's* instead of *hers, yours* and *theirs* (the possessive pronoun forms, as in *This pen is yours; that one is hers and those blue ones are theirs*). Here the confusion is not between existing word-forms but may be due to hypercorrection, i.e. using an incorrect form based on a convention that applies in other similar contexts, in this case the *'s* indicating possession when used with nouns.

This kind of sound–spelling mix-up also occurs with the contracted forms of *should have* (*should've*) and *would have* (*would've*), where people sometimes write *should of* and *would of*. I've also heard it pronounced that way. The Spoken BNC2014 contains 21 examples of *should of* followed by a past participle (e.g. *I should of brought my camera out / he should of called her a month ago*), though it is not clear if these are conscious or accidental transcriptions.

INFORMATION ADD-ON

In 2006, the UK *Mirror* newspaper accused the department store Marks and Spencer of a 'grammar blunder' for confusing *ones* (pronoun, as in *large ones*) and *one's* (possessive determiner, as in *pay one's taxes*) (https://www.mirror.co.uk/news/uk-news/ms-in-grammar-blunder-654467).

The newspaper's website later reported on a nine-year-old girl who had recorded 15 apostrophe 'howlers' publicly visible in her northern English town, which included non-standard plurals in signs advertising items such as *pie's* and *sandwich's*. Note the strong words *blunder* and *howler* (https://www.mirror.co.uk/news/uk-news/nine-year-old-spotted-15-6713651).

For many years, Britain had its own *Apostrophe Protection Society*, dedicated to preserving traditionally correct uses of the apostrophe. It often made the headlines and survived until 2019, when its founder admitted defeat in the face of public laziness and ignorance and closed it down for good (https://www.bbc.co.uk/news/world-us-canada-50692797).

Punctuation, like other features of grammar, changes over time in the hands of its users. Even before the invention of email and social media, punctuation was changing and becoming less dense in texts. This extract from the opening dedication of the eighteenth-century novel *The Life and Opinions of Tristram Shandy, Gentleman*, by Laurence Sterne, now appears over-punctuated to our modern eye. The brackets, dashes and semi-colons make it more, not less difficult for the twenty-first century reader to follow the syntax:

> I humbly beg, Sir, that you will honour this book, by taking it—(not under your Protection,—it must protect itself, but)—into the country with you; where, if I am ever told, it has made you smile; or can conceive it has beguiled you of one moment's pain—I shall think myself as happy as a minister of state;—perhaps much happier than any one (one only excepted) that I have read or heard of.
>
> (Sterne, 2009)

Change in grammatical conventions is inevitable, but it is often accompanied by heated debate, and punctuation is no exception. In the easy-going world of personal emails and social media postings, punctuation reflects the democratisation of grammar, freeing it from the stifling orthodoxy of the grammar police. On the other hand, there is a good argument for adhering to grammatical conventions, including punctuation conventions, in formal writing such as scientific, official and academic documents, where clarity of expression and lack of ambiguity are paramount.

PRONOUNS: NOT SO CLOSED AFTER ALL?

Until about 50 years ago, most people would not have objected to sentences such as:

*Any person knows that **he** will be faced with important decisions in his career.*
*Every student must bring **his** identity card to the examination room.*

People simply assumed that *he* and *his* meant everyone, male or female. I was one of them. However, in the last part of the twentieth century, things changed, and a greater sense of equality of the sexes meant that ingenuity was needed to make the pronoun system more egalitarian. Several things happened: In speaking, people began to say *he or she* and *she or he*; in writing, people started to write *she/he, he/she* or *(s)he*. People also began simply to use the plural *they* to refer to an individual of either sex, so that *One student was caught smuggling their mobile phone into the exam room* is now perfectly normal and acceptable. This use of *they/their* in this way sometimes annoys traditionalists, but in fact if you look it up in the *Oxford English Dictionary*, there are examples going back hundreds of years, including in the writing of the highly regarded nineteenth-century essayist John Ruskin. Another way in which *they/their* can be used is when a person does not wish to be associated with either male or female gender. The science journalist Annalee Newitz, who writes regularly for *New Scientist* magazine prefers to be described in the following way: 'Their latest novel is *The Future of Another Timeline* and they are co-host of the Hugo-nominated podcast *Our Opinions are Correct*' (*New Scientist* 6 June 2020: 21).

In some dialects of British, North American and Caribbean English, you will hear variations on *themselves*, such as *themself, theirselves*, or *theirself*, and *ourself* as a variant of *ourselves*. These forms too are very old, going back hundreds of years. Many people consider them non-standard (including the grammar-checker on my computer), but the linguist Nancy Stern has argued that *ourself* and *themself* can be used effectively to neutralise the singular–plural distinction when the situation demands it (Stern 2019), and in Canadian English, *themself* is considered an appropriate gender-neutral pronoun covering *himself* and *herself* in the wording of legislation (Revell et al. 1994).

But the personal pronoun closed system has been subject to more than just a rearrangement of the existing words or the inclusion of what were non-standard forms to fill gaps. Recently, forms such as *ze* (pronounced 'zee') and *hir* (rhyming with 'here') have become candidates for expressing gender neutrality, so a sentence such as *Ze values hir privacy* could be equivalent to either *he* or *she values his* or *her privacy*. These proposed new forms have not become widely accepted – time will tell if they do become a new norm. If they do, then the closed system of personal pronouns will have opened its doors to admit new members. And, who knows, the pronoun *one* (as in *One must be careful how one chooses one's friends*) may slide into oblivion if speakers no longer feel a need for it, or feel it is too posh or stigmatised in some other way. Nothing is guaranteed to be permanent in grammar.

> **CORPUS EVIDENCE**
>
> If we separate the BNC1994 into three time periods according to when the texts date from (1960–1974, 1975–1984 and 1985–1993), we can see a steady decline in the frequency of the personal pronoun *one* (Figure 8.3).

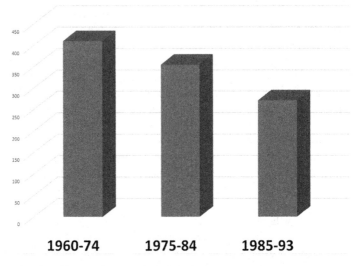

personal pronoun *one* in BNC1994 (per 1m words)

Figure 8.3 Personal pronoun *one*.

ADVERBIALS: WHY DO PEOPLE GET AFFRONTED?

English adverbials feature in the National Curriculum at primary school level in the UK and in Australia. If you are a school teacher in the UK, you might find yourself embroiled in debates about fronted adverbials (see Chapter 2). Fronted adverbials seem to be one of those features that stir controversy, centring around the wisdom or otherwise of teaching young children this kind of terminology. In 2017, the British *Guardian* newspaper website had the headline: 'BATTLE ON THE ADVERBIALS FRONT'. The piece began:

> This morning, more than half a million primary children will take a test that may ask them to identify the grammatical label for the two-word phrase at the start of this paragraph. Could you do it? If you are unable to recognise this as a 'fronted adverbial' then you will have fallen short on knowledge expected of 10- and 11-year-olds in the controversial spelling, punctuation and grammar (Spag) tests.
>
> (https://www.theguardian.com/education/2017/may/09/fronted-adverbials-sats-grammar-test-primary)

The article went on to refer to 'a fierce debate' over these grammar requirements. Fronted adverbials feature regularly in discussions about children's writing (see mentions in the chapters in Bushnell et al. 2020). Fronted adverbials have found their way to the front line of the public battleground over grammar. Subjects, verbs and objects get off lightly in comparison.

TELLING IT LIKE IT IS

Like is a versatile word and it is very frequent; it was number 12 in the spoken frequency list on p. 76. In sentence grammar, it is a verb or a preposition. People also use it as a conjunction to connect clauses:

*He is **like** a father to me.* (preposition)
*She goes to work **like** I do, by bike.* (conjunction)

In this last example, connecting clauses, purists might insist on *as* instead of *like*. But the uses of *like* which are most controversial are best seen in this extract from the Spoken BNC2014:

[the speakers are talking about a 3D film which speaker 0529 had been to see]

<S0529>   yeah no it was it was really long and I was **like** is this over yet? and <laughs>

<S0530>   it wasn't really about the plot

<S0529>   but it was good in 3D

<S0530>   it was more about yeah

<S0529>   yeah

<S0530>   that graphics

<S0529>   it was the only film I'd enjoyed seeing in 3D **like like** I actually felt **like** it enhanced the experience

<S0530>   oh really?

<S0529>   yeah everything else was just <unclear>

<S0530>   was the animation **like** beautiful?

<S0529>   yeah it was crazy it was **like** you could touch it **like** oh my god

<S0530>   wow

(Spoken BNC2014 SXSM)

There are two very common uses of *like* in the extract. The first is in the words *and I was **like** is this over yet?* and ***like** oh my god*, where the speaker is reporting their thoughts during the film. The second is seen in the lines: *was the animation **like** beautiful? / yeah it was crazy it was **like** you could touch it*, where *like* seems to focus on important words and phrases, as if shining a light on them (*beautiful, you could touch it*).

The 'reported thoughts' use of *I was like* is paralleled by many examples where the speaker is quoting their own words or what someone else has said, as in this extract:

[talking about a neighbour who wanted to borrow a garden strimmer, referred to as *the machine*]

<S0441>   no yeah he he text back but I didn't get it so he knocked on the door and **was like** can I borrow the machine? and **I was like** yeah that's fine **he was like** I'm just going to the gym so I'll be back in two hours **I was like** okay er to use it **I was like** that's fine **he was like** erm <short pause> will you help me do it? and **I was like** yeah that's fine

(Spoken BNC2014 S2AJ)

In my 2021 book on grammar, I noted that the Spoken BNC2014 returns more than 9,000 hits in a search for *I/(s)he was like*. I reduced these to a random sample of 200 examples and found that 177 of them introduced direct speech reports, as in the example above (McCarthy 2021: 97–8). Two linguists who studied the use of the *be like* construction (Romaine and Lange 1991) showed that it does not necessarily mean the speaker is quoting their own or someone else's words. *I was like* can be used to represent the speaker's thoughts, emotions or stance towards a situation, a sort of 'dialogue with the self'.

In Irish English, *like* often comes at the end of what someone says as a marker of 'that's what I want to say', as in these examples from the LCIE corpus (see also Clancy 2005):

<$1> Why didn't you tell me yesterday?
<$2> I keep forgettin' **like**.

(LCIE6778887)

<$2> You can't have a Dalmatian* in a housing estate. You just can't do it **like**.
<$6> No.
<$2> Cos they're too energetic.

(LCIE6778890) [*breed of dog]

The use of *like* generally seems to have been on the increase in the 20 years that separate the BNC1994 and the Spoken BNC2014. According to the BNClab, a free online facility that gives statistics about words in the two versions of the BNC, there is an almost three times greater use of *like* in the 2014 version, with a predominance of use among younger people in the teens and twenties and thirties (http://corpora.la ncs.ac.uk/bnclab/search). As is often the case, target groups for expressions of annoyance or condemnation tend to be the young, the uneducated or other marginalised groups in society, which Elizabeth Petersen points to in her book on 'bad English' (Peterson 2020).

The Internet is not entirely intolerant of the use of *like*, and most sites giving advice on it stress that it is very informal and should be avoided in formal situations. However, it is easy to find online references to it as an *annoying* habit, a *bad* habit, an *epidemic*, a *verbal tick*, *ridiculous*, something that *infects* speech patterns, something that indicates *a lazy mind*, something that should be *erased* from usage, something that makes people *sound so unintelligent*, a habit that should be *curbed*, and advice on *how to stop saying 'like' and immediately sound smarter.*

A blog on the subject of reported speech sums up this kind of disquiet: 'For many, the use of *like* to introduce reported speech is a bugbear, something to be ranted about and, if possible, stopped!' (https://www.lexicallab.com/2017/02/grammar-curiosities-1-reported-speech/). The blogger rejects such condemnation and argues for its use as a creative reporting strategy, and one study that looked at speech reporting on social media posts with expressions such as *I was like* and *she goes* concluded that the expressions 'animate and modally enrich reported speech' (Wikström 2014).

REFLECTION POINT

In 2010, the Oscar-winning actor Emma Thompson was interviewed for the UK magazine *Radio Times*. She was quoted as saying that slang used by youngsters made her feel 'insane':

'I went to give a talk at my old school and the girls were all doing their "likes" and "innits?" and "it ain'ts", which drives me insane,' she told the Radio Times.
'I told them "Just don't do it. Because it makes you sound stupid and you're not stupid. There is the necessity to have two languages – one that you use with your mates and the other that you need in any official capacity."'
Ian McNeilly, Director of the UK National Association for Teaching of English said:
'I agree with Emma Thompson. The danger of young people using language like that is that people assume they're somehow stupid. And that isn't true.'

(https://www.mirror.co.uk/3am/celebrity-news/emma-thompson-has-blasted-the-sloppy-way-250340)

Comments on *like* from both sides of the fence are an example of the frequent disconnect between what academics say about grammar and what the public thinks and says. Academics and professional grammarians are, in the main, tolerant of changes in usage and stress the importance of awareness of the different situations in which something might be appropriate or inappropriate. They also point to the relationship between language and identity; if you use *like* in the way we have described, it can act as a badge of membership of a group (e.g. teenagers, students). If you are an outsider to that group, you may get irritated by the group's use of language. But we should never condemn as stupidity or ignorance the genuine feelings of ordinary people, whether we are talking about the groups that use *like* or the people who condemn them for using it. Rather, we should make an effort to understand why people use language in the ways they do, and why other people react in the ways they do. Language change is inevitable, it reflects social change, and social change can be unnerving, challenging and upsetting.

THE LINGUISTIC LANDSCAPE: BEING CREATIVE WITH GRAMMAR

An important feature of the linguistic landscape is advertising. Advertising slogans have to be short and eye-catching, something often achieved by images and animations, whether on traditional or digital billboards. Apart from the images, grammar also has a role, with some of the cleverest advertising slogans deliberately breaking the grammatical conventions. Here are some recent examples:

1   *Apple – Think Different.*
2   *Because you're worth it.*
3   *I'm lovin' it.*
4   *Betcha can't eat just one.*
5   *Look good, feel good, live good.*

Number (1), the Apple™ slogan, breaks the standard convention that a lexical verb should be modified by an adverb (*think differently*), just as in (5), for Starest™ skin care products, standard grammar would require *live well*. *Verb + adjective* seems to be an effective eye-catching pattern, whether the grammar is absorbed consciously or unconsciously by the reader.

In (2), the slogan of L'Oréal Paris™, we have a subordinate clause with no main clause. The reader 'fills in' the missing main clause (e.g. 'buy L'Oréal products for yourself because you are worth it / you deserve them'). Example (3) (the McDonald's™ slogan) and (4) (advertising Lay's™ potato chips/crisps) both use dialect pronunciation effects (*lovin', betcha'*) to suggest that the ad is speaking to you, not writing, and speaking in a very informal grammar, like a friend, with the use of continuous *be* + *-ing* in *I'm lovin'*, and ellipsis in *betcha* ('I bet you'). The Irish linguist Joan O'Sullivan has shown how effective the use of Irish English can be in advertising (O'Sullivan 2020).

These instances of non-standard grammar are generally either not noticed or praised as clever and creative. They are not seen as evidence of the decline of public morals or social standards and do not generate moral panics, probably because they are associated with an educated, middle-class, creative sector of society that works in the advertising profession. They are not seen as the grammar of lazy teenagers or social media addicts.

CONCLUSION

I have tried in this chapter, and throughout this book, not to condemn anyone's grammar, or to take sides in the battle over grammar in our schools. Whether your grammar is influenced by your age, your social class, your peer group or the place where you grew up, whether English is your first language or a second language, whether you speak the long-established English of countries such as the UK, Canada or New Zealand, or one of the independent new English varieties, or just use English as a communicative tool in business or travel, you have choices when it comes to grammar. You can adhere to standards of correctness based on models such as the educated, school-curriculum standard of countries where English is a first or dominant language, or you can take a different approach and proudly wear your dialect or variety of English and its grammar as a badge of membership, and swap around and use grammar in different ways according to the situation. You can also choose to pooh-pooh grammar altogether and throw this book in the bin. However, choices are always more satisfying if they are made on the basis of knowledge, evidence and awareness of what the choices imply, where they came from and where they may take you. To make the right choices for yourself with regard to grammar, you need the basics. That is all this book can give you. The rest is up to you.

FURTHER READING

Crystal, D. 2006. *The Fight for English. How Language Pundits Ate, Shot and Left*. **Oxford: Oxford University Press.**
Any book by linguist and broadcaster David Crystal is worth reading because of his clear, humorous style and his years of distinguished scholarship, but this one is particularly interesting if you want to read more about public controversies and attitudes to grammar of the kind raised in this chapter.

Trudgill, P. 2016. Respecting ordinary language. In *Dialect Matters: Respecting Vernacular Language*. **Cambridge: Cambridge University Press, 104–121.**
Peter Trudgill's writings show enormous and non-patronising respect for the language of ordinary people, the language that was so ignored over the centuries by prescriptive grammarians. This chapter of his book includes discussion of like and criticises the influence of powerful groups in society.

Scollon, R. and Scollon, S. W. 2003. *Discourses in Place: Language in the Material World*. **Abingdon, Oxon: Routledge.**
This is a great and very accessible introduction to the study of language in public places and includes discussion of how grammar and standardised language has been used over the centuries as a means of social control in the public domain. It is the best source to understand the linguistic landscape.

GLOSSARY OF GRAMMAR TERMS

adverbial
The phrase in a clause which indicates the surrounding circumstances. In the clause _yesterday_ he left _in a hurry_, _yesterday_ and _in a hurry_ are adverbials.

affirmative
With a positive meaning; the opposite of negative in a clause, e.g. _he resigned_ (affirmative); _he didn't resign_ (negative).

agent, agentless
The person who does the action in a passive voice clause, e.g. _I was contacted by an old school friend_. An agentless passive does not mention the doer, e.g. _He was arrested._

apostrophe
A punctuation mark like a superscript comma, used to indicate possession (_Jim's car_), or missing letters (_isn't, who's_).

articles
_A(n)_ is the indefinite article, _the_ is the definite article, using no article is the zero article.

auxiliary verb
_Be_, _do_ and _have_ can be used as auxiliary verbs to support main verbs, e.g. _she is working_; _I don't like this_; _they have left._

base form
The form of a word with no endings added (e.g. _look, eat, book, computer_).

case
The case of a pronoun tells us if it is subject (e.g. *she, we, they*) or object (*her, us, them*) or possessive (*my/mine, his, your/yours*).

clause
A grammatical unit that includes a verb phrase.

cleft, *it*-cleft, *wh*-cleft
When a single event is split into two clauses, e.g. *it was Harry who broke the vase; what we need is greater clarity.*

comparative
A comparative indicates that someone or something has more of a quality than something or someone else, e.g. *she is <u>taller</u> than her sister; that book was <u>more interesting</u> than the other one.*

complement
Verbs such as *be, seem, look, taste* do not take objects – they take complements. In *she is a doctor*, 'a doctor' is the complement.

compound
Two or more words fused together into one unit of meaning, e.g. *car park, headphones, wastepaper basket, long-lasting.*

concord
How the subject and verb agree in number and person, e.g. *<u>he likes</u> horror films; <u>we like</u> comedies.*

conditional
Subordinate clause or sentence that sets conditions for something, e.g. *<u>if it rains</u>, we'll stay indoors; assume I'll be there <u>unless you hear otherwise</u>.*

continuous or progressive aspect
A way of looking at an event from within it, with no reference to its start or end, e.g. *he <u>is</u> work<u>ing</u>; they <u>were</u> mend<u>ing</u> the wall.*

coordinating conjunctions
Words that join two grammatical units of equal status: *and, but, or.*

correlative
Refers to structures such as *either ... or, neither ... nor, both ... and.*

declarative
See **mood**.

demonstrative
This, that, these and *those* are demonstratives.

deontic modality
Using modal verbs to refer to degrees of necessity or desirability.

derivation, prefixes and suffixes
The process of making new words from existing ones by adding prefixes (e.g. *reform*, *abnormal*) and suffixes (*reformation*, *abnormality*).

determiner
Word that specifies something about a noun, e.g. *this book*, *my father*, *some food*, *a bus*, *the moon*.

direct and indirect object
In *Ken gave Laura a book*, Laura is the end-recipient of the book. Laura is the indirect object. The book is the direct object.

ellipsis
The absence of grammatical items which would be compulsory in formal writing, e.g. *Going out tonight?* means the same as *Are you going out tonight?*

epistemic modality
Using modal verbs to refer to degrees of possibility or certainty.

etymology
The study of the origin and history of words.

generic pronoun
Using a pronoun to refer to people in general, e.g. *you have to pass a test to get a driving licence*; *one should always be polite*.

gerund
The *-ing* form of a verb when it is acting as a noun, e.g. *Swimming keeps you fit.*

imperative
See **mood**.

indicative
See **mood**.

infinitive
The *to-* form of a verb, e.g. *to eat, to look, to be or not to be.*

interjection
Word or expression indicating a strong reaction, e.g. *wow! oh no! gosh! oops!*

interrogative
See **mood**.

lexis, lexical
Referring to the vocabulary of a language.

lingua franca
A language used for communication between parties when that language is not the first language of any party (e.g. a Swedish speaker and a Japanese speaker using English to communicate with each other).

main clause
An independent clause that can stand on its own and make sense. A sentence must have at least one main clause.

modal verbs
Modal verbs are verbs such as *can, could, shall, should, will, would, might, may, ought.*

mood, indicative, imperative, subjunctive
Different ways of referring to reality. Indicative mood is concerned with facts and truth (*She's a teacher; Did he phone you?*). *She's a teacher* is declarative; *Did he phone you?* is interrogative. *Sit down!* is **imperative** (concerned with commands). *Were we to win, we would get a £5,000 prize* is subjunctive (it is unreal and hypothetical).

morphology, morphemes
The study of how words are composed of units of meaning; the morpheme is the smallest unit of meaning.

non-finite clause
Clause with a verb with no subject in the -ing, past participle or to-infinitive form, e.g. *Hoping for a quick reply, I texted her at once.*

object
The 'receiver' of an action. In *Ken ate the pie, the pie* is the object (see also direct and indirect object).

orthography
The writing system of a language.

past participle
The third part of a verb (e.g. *take, took, taken; drink, drank, drunk).*

perfect aspect
A way of looking at an event in relation to the present or to another point in the past, e.g. *she has arrived; they had sold their house.*

phonology
The sound system of a language.

phrase
A grammatical unit composed of words which has a function in the composition of a clause (e.g. *the subject phrase, the verb phrase*).

pre- and post-modifiers
Words that come before (pre-) and after (post-) the noun in a noun phrase, e.g. *the old man who visited her; two distant relatives of mine.*

preposition
Small word that specifies something about a noun or pronoun such as time (*in summer, at the weekend*), place (*under the table, on the corner*) identity (*head of government, assistant to the director*), direction (*towards Madrid, over the river*), etc.

present participle
The -ing form of a verb when it is used with be, e.g. *he's waiting; the kids are playing.*

pronoun
Word that substitutes for a noun or noun phrase, e.g. *we, they, it, us, him, she, themselves, someone*.

reflexive
Refers to pronouns such as *myself, yourself, themselves*.

register
The use of language depending on the situation, e.g. *the registers of journalism and academic writing are different*.

relative clause
Clause introduced by *who, which, whom, whose, that* or Ø (zero) attached to a noun or commenting on a sentence, e.g. *the woman who stole the car; a book that I borrowed; he failed the exam, which was a pity*.

relative pronoun
Words such as *who, which, whom, that*, used to introduce a relative clause.

reported clause
Clause that is the object of a verb that reports speech or mental states, e.g. *She said she would do it; I knew it was wrong*.

sentence
A grammatical unit that includes at least one main clause.

simple aspect
A way of looking at an event as an outsider or observer, e.g. *she sings; I worked; they bought a camper-van*.

subject
The 'doer' of an action. In *Ken ate the pie*, Ken is the subject.

subjunctive
See **mood**.

subordinate clause
A dependent clause that cannot stand on its own and make complete sense (e.g. *if it rains; because she was ill*). It needs a main clause with it to make complete sense.

subordinating conjunction
Word that introduces a subordinate clause (e.g. *if*, *when*, *before*, *since*, *as*, *because*).

superlative
A superlative indicates that something has more of a quality than any other person or thing in a group, e.g. *the tallest* building in the city; *the most intelligent* child in the class.

syntax
The grammatical conventions for arranging words in sentences.

transitive, intransitive and di-transitive
If a verb does not need an object it is intransitive (*she laughed*); If a verb needs an object it is transitive (*I love roses*); if it needs two objects it is di-transitive (*they gave the boy a medal*).

voice, active and passive
Active voice means the grammatical subject of the clause and the 'doer' are the same (*Frankie wrote the book*). Passive voice is when the psychological object becomes the grammatical subject (*the book was written [by Frankie]*).

word
A unit of meaning consisting of at least one morpheme.

word class
All words belong to classes (e.g. noun, adjective, preposition).

REFERENCES

Ahulu, S. 1998. Grammatical variation in international English. *English Today* 14 (4): 19–25.

Allen, E. E. and Mason, A. T. 1939. *An English Grammar of Function. Book II.* London: Edward Arnold and Co.

Anonymous. 1911. *On the Terminology of Grammar: Being the Report of the Joint Committee on Grammatical Terminology.* Revised. London: John Murray.

Banjo, A. 1997. Aspects of the syntax of Nigerian English. In E. W. Schneider (ed.), *Englishes around the World: Studies in Honour of Manfred Görlach.* Volume 2: Caribbean, Africa, Asia, Australasia. Amsterdam: John Benjamins Publishing Company, 85–95.

Bernard, N. 1999. The fall and rise of grammar in the Australian English curriculum: Factors in a continuum of change. *La Trobe papers in linguistics* 10: 119–157. Retrieved from http://arrow.latrobe.edu.au:8080/vital/access/manager/Repository/latrobe:33084.

Bloomfield, L. 1933/1935. *Language.* Revised edition. London: George Allen and Unwin.

Brazil, D. 1995. *A Grammar of Speech.* Oxford: Oxford University Press.

Bruthiaux, P. 1995. The rise and fall of the semicolon: English punctuation theory and English teaching practice. *Applied Linguistics* 16 (1): 1–14.

Bushnell, A., Gill, A. and Waugh, D. (eds) 2020. *Mastering Writing at Greater Depth: A Guide for Primary Teaching.* London: Sage.

Bybee, J. 2010. *Language, Usage and Cognition.* Cambridge: Cambridge University Press.

Carter, R. 1997. *Investigating English Discourse.* London: Routledge.

Carter, R. 1999. Standard grammars, spoken grammars: Some educational implications. In T. Bex and R. Watts (eds), *Standard English: The Widening Debate.* London: Routledge, 149–166.

Carter, R. A. and McCarthy, M. J. 1999. The English *get*-passive in spoken discourse: Description and implications for an interpersonal grammar. *English Language and Linguistics,* 3 (1): 41–58.

Carter, R. A. and McCarthy, M. J. 1997. *Exploring Spoken English*. Cambridge: Cambridge University Press.

Carter, R. and McCarthy, M. J. 2006. *Cambridge Grammar of English*. Cambridge: Cambridge University Press.

Cheshire, J. 1999. Spoken standard English. In T. Bex and R. Watts (eds), *Standard English: The Widening Debate*. London: Routledge, 129–148.

Chomsky, N. 1957. *Syntactic Structures*. The Hague: Mouton.

Chomsky, N. 1959. Review of *Verbal Behavior* by B. F. Skinner. *Language* 35 (1): 26–58.

Chomsky, N. 1964. The development of grammar in child language: Discussion. *Monographs of the Society for Research in Child Development* 29 (1): 35–42.

Chomsky, N. 1965. *Aspects of the Theory of Syntax*. Cambridge, MA: The MIT Press.

Clancy, B. 2005. You're fat. You'll eat them all: Politeness strategies in family discourse. In: A. Barron and K. Schneider (eds), *The Pragmatics of Irish English*. Berlin: Walter de Gruyter, 177–199.

Cop, M. and Hatfield, H. 2017. An athletes [sic] performance: Can a possessive apostrophe predict success? *English Today* 33 (3): 39–45.

Corrigan, K. 2011. Grammatical variation in Irish English. *English Today* 27 (2): 39–46.

Croft, W. and Cruse, D. 2004. *Cognitive Linguistics*. Cambridge: Cambridge University Press.

Dent, S. 2020. Does it have the end this way? The kids have killed the full stop. *The Sunday Times*, 30 August: 24.

Evans, V. and Green, M. 2015. *Cognitive Linguistics: An Introduction*. New York: Routledge.

Everett, D. L. 2017. Grammar came later: Triality of patterning and the gradual evolution of language. *Journal of Neurolinguistics* 43: 133–165.

Farr, F. and O'Keeffe, A. 2002. Would as a hedging device in an Irish context: An intra-varietal comparison of institutionalised spoken interaction. In R. Reppen, S. Fitzmaurice and D. Biber (eds), *Using Corpora to Explore Linguistic Variation*. Amsterdam: John Benjamins, 25–48.

Fries, C. C. 1945. *Teaching and Learning English as a Foreign Language*. Ann Arbor: The University of Michigan Press.

Fries, C. C. 1952. *The Structure of English*. New York: Harcourt, Brace and Company.

Gannon, S. and Sawyer, W. 2007. 'Whole language' and moral panic in Australia. *International Journal of Progressive Education* 3 (2): 30–51.

Glaze, B. 2015. Michael Gove gives 'patronising' grammar lessons to Ministry of Justice staff. *The Mirror* 22 June 2015. Accessed at: https://www.mirror.co.uk/news/uk-news/michael-gove-gives-patronising-grammar-5926858.

Grice, E. 2013. The glamour of grammar: An object lesson. *The Telegraph* 13 April 2013. Accessed at: https://www.telegraph.co.uk/education/ 9987974/The-glamour-ofgrammar-an-object-lesson.html.

Gwynne, N. M. 2013. *Gwynne's Grammar*. London: Ebury Press.

Halliday, M. A. K. 1961. Categories of the theory of grammar. *Word* 17 (2): 241–292.

Halliday, M. A. K. 1967. Notes on transitivity and theme in English: Part 1. *Journal of Linguistics* 3 (1): 37–81.

Halliday, M. A. K. 1967/2007. Linguistics and the teaching of English. In J. J. Webster (ed.), *Language and Education*. Volume 9 in the *Collected Works of M. A. K. Halliday*. London: Continuum, 25–34.

Halliday, M. A. K. 1978. *Language as Social Semiotic: The Social Interpretation of Language and Meaning*. London: Edward Arnold.

Halliday, M. A. K. 1996. On grammar and grammatics. In R. Hasan, C. Cloran and D. G. Butt (eds), *Functional Descriptions: Theory in Practice*. Amsterdam: John Benjamins, 1–38.

Harris, J. 1993. The grammar of Irish English. In J. Milroy and L. Milroy (eds), *Real English*. Harlow: Longman, 139–186.

Hawking, S. 2001. *The Universe in a Nutshell*. London: Bantam Books.

Hazen, K., Hamilton, S. and Vacovsky, S. 2011. The fall of demonstrative *them*: Evidence from Appalachia. *English World-Wide* 32 (1): 74–103.

Hickey, R. 2007. Southern Irish English. In D. Britain (ed.), *Language in the British Isles*. Cambridge: Cambridge University Press, 135–151.

Hopper, P. 1988. Discourse analysis: Grammar and critical theory in the 1980s. *Profession*: 18–24. Retrieved from http://www.jstor.org/stable/25595414.

Hopper, P. 1996. Some recent trends in grammaticalization. *Annual Review of Anthropology* 25: 217–236.

Hopper, P. 2011. Emergent grammar and temporality in interactional linguistics. In P. Auer and S. Pfänder (eds), *Constructions: Emerging and Emergent*. Berlin: Walter de Gruyter, 22–44.

Horton, S. and Bingle, B. 2014. *Lessons in Teaching Grammar in Primary Schools*. London: Sage.

Hudson, R. and Walmsley, J. 2005. The English Patient: English Grammar and teaching in the twentieth century. *Journal of linguistics* 41 (3): 593–622.

Hunston, S. and Francis, G. 2000. *Pattern Grammar: A Corpus-driven Approach to the Lexical Grammar of English*. Amsterdam: John Benjamins.

Jones, D. 2017. Talking about talk: Reviewing oracy in English primary education. *Early Child Development and Care* 187 (3–4):498–508.

Kamm, O. 2015. Ignore the 'good grammar' crowd and your prose will be better for it. *The Spectator* 25 June 2015. Accessed at: https://blogs.specta tor.co.uk/2015/06/ignore-the-good-grammar-crowd-and-your-prose-will-be-better-for-it/.

Kolln, M. and Hancock, C. 2005. The story of English grammar in United States schools. *English Teaching: Practice and Critique* 4 (3): 11–31.

Landry, R. and Bourhis, R. Y. 1997. Linguistic landscape and ethnolinguistic vitality: An empirical study. *Journal of Language and Social Psychology* 16 (1): 23–49.

Langacker, R. 1987. *Foundations of Cognitive Grammar. Volume 1. Theoretical Prerequisites*. Stanford: Stanford University Press.

Langacker, R. W. 2009. Cognitive grammar. In D. Sandra, J.-O. Östman and J. Verschueren (eds), *Cognition and Pragmatics*. Amsterdam: John Benjamins, 78–85.

Lange, C. and Leuckert, S. 2020. *Corpus Linguistics for World Englishes*. Abingdon, Oxon: Routledge.

Leech, G. 2000. Grammars of spoken English: New outcomes of corpus-oriented research. *Language Learning* 50 (4): 675–724.

Little, G. 1986. The ambivalent apostrophe. *English Today* 8: 15–17.

Lowth, R. 1762/1799. *A Short Introduction to English Grammar*. Philadelphia: R. Aitken.

Malinowski, B. 1923. The problem of meaning in primitive languages. In C. K. Ogden and I. A. Richards (eds), *The Meaning of Meaning*. London: Kegan Paul, Trench, Trubner, 296–336.

Matthews, P. 2001. *A Short History of Structural Linguistics*. Cambridge: Cambridge University Press.

McCarthy, M. J. 1994. It, this and that. In R. M. Coulthard (ed.), *Advances in Written Text Analysis*. London: Routledge, 266–275.

McCarthy, M. J. 1998. *Spoken Language and Applied Linguistics*. Cambridge: Cambridge University Press.

McCarthy, M. J. 2002. Good listenership made plain: British and American non-minimal response tokens in everyday conversation. In R. Reppen, S. Fitzmaurice and D. Biber (eds), *Using Corpora to Explore Linguistic Variation*. Amsterdam: John Benjamins, 49–71.

McCarthy, M. J. 2003. Talking back: 'small' interactional response tokens in everyday conversation. *Research on Language in Social Interaction* 36 (1): 33–63.

McCarthy, M. J. 2021. *Innovations and Challenges in Grammar*. Abingdon, Oxon: Routledge.

McCarthy, M. J. and Carter, R. 1997. Grammar, tails and affect: Constructing expressive choices in discourse. *Text and Talk* 17: 405–429.

Milroy, J. and Milroy, L. 1999. *Authority in English: Investigating Standard English*. 3rd edition. London: Routledge.

Mitchell, T. F 1957. The language of buying and selling in Cyrenaica: A situational statement. *Hespéris* XLIV: 31–71.

Murphy, L. 2018. *The Prodigal Tongue: The Love-Hate Relationship Between American and British English*. New York: Penguin.

Nesfield, J. C. 1920. *Outline of English Grammar*. Revised edition. London: Macmillan.

Nevalainen, T. and Van Ostade, I. 2006. Standardisation. In R. Hogg and D. Denison (eds), *A History of the English Language*. Cambridge: Cambridge University Press, 271–311.

O'Keeffe, A. and Amador Moreno, C. P. 2009. The pragmatics of the *be + after + V-ing* construction in Irish English. *Intercultural Pragmatics* 6 (4): 517–534.

O'Sullivan, J. 2020. *Corpus Linguistics and the Analysis of Sociolinguistic Change: Language Variety and Ideology in Advertising*. Abingdon, Oxon: Routledge.

Palmer, F. R. 1968. *Selected Papers of J. R. Firth 1952–59*. London: Longmans, Green and Co.

Palmer, H. E. 1924. *A Grammar of Spoken English on a Strictly Phonetic Basis*. Cambridge: W. Heffer and Sons.

Penhallurick, R. 2007. English in Wales. In D. Britain (ed.), *Language in the British Isles*. Cambridge: Cambridge University Press, 152–170.

Peterson, E. 2020. *Making Sense of 'Bad English': An Introduction to Language Attitudes and Ideologies*. Abingdon, Oxon: Routledge.

Quirk, R., Greenbaum, S., Leech, G. and Svartvik, J. 1985. *A Comprehensive Grammar of the English Language*. Harlow: Longman.

Revell, D. L., Schuh, C. and Moisan, M. 1994. 'Themself' and nonsexist style in Canadian legislative drafting. *English Today* 10 (1): 10–17.

Romaine, S. and Lange, D. 1991. The Use of *like* as a marker of reported speech and thought: A case of grammaticalization in progress. *American Speech* 66 (3): 227–279.

Saussure, F. de 1916/2011. *Course in General Linguistics*. Translated by Wade Baskin. New York: Columbia University Press.

Schaffer, D. 2010. Old whine online: Prescriptive grammar blogs on the Internet. *English Today* 26 (4): 23–28.

Schiffrin, D. 1987. *Discourse Markers*. Cambridge: Cambridge University Press.

Schmid, H.-J. and Ungerer, F. 2011. Cognitive linguistics. In J. Simpson (ed.), *The Routledge Handbook of Applied Linguistics*. London: Routledge, 611–624.

Schwyter, J. R. 2016. *Dictating to the Mob: The History of the BBC Advisory Committee on Spoken English*. Oxford: Oxford University Press.

Scollon, R. and Scollon, S. W. 2003. *Discourses in place: Language in the material world*. London: Routledge.

Sinclair, J. McH. 1991. *Corpus, Concordance, Collocation*. Oxford: Oxford University Press.

Skinner, B. F. 1957. *Verbal Behavior*. London: Methuen & Co.

Stern, N. 2019. Ourself and themself: Grammar as expressive choice. *Lingua* 226: 35–52.

Sterne, L. 2009. *The Life and Opinions of Tristram Shandy, Gentleman*. London: Wordsworth.

Tagliamonte, S. A. 2013. *Roots of English: Exploring the History of Dialects*. Cambridge: Cambridge University Press.

Tagliamonte, S. and Hudson, R. 1999. Be like et al. beyond America: The quotative system in British and Canadian youth. *Journal of Sociolinguistics* 3: 147–172.

Tamaredo, I. 2018. Pronoun omission in high-contact varieties of English. *English World-Wide* 39 (1): 85–110.

The Kingman Report. 1988. *English Today* 4 (4): 15–23.

Thompson, K. 1998. *Moral Panics*. London: Routledge.

Tomasello, M. 2003. *Constructing a Language: A Usage-based Theory of Language Acquisition*. Cambridge, MA: Harvard University Press.

Trudgill, P. 2016. *Dialect Matters: Respecting Vernacular Language*. Cambridge: Cambridge University Press.

Van Rooy, B. 2013. Corpus linguistic work on Black South African English. *English Today* 29 (1): 10–15.

Wikström, P. 2014. & she was like 'O_O': Animation of reported speech on Twitter. *Nordic Journal of English Studies* 13 (3): 83–111.

Yamaguchi, T. and Deterding, D. (eds) 2016. *English in Malaysia. Current Use and Status*. Leiden: Brill.

INDEX

Aarts, B. 98
active voice 36, 107–8
adjectives 27, 31, 55, 70–1, 133
adverbials 33, 35, 48, 72–3, 145, 180–1
adverbs 26, 48, 55, 72–3, 162
affirmative 32, 68, 96
agent 37, 38, 63
agentless passive 37
agreement 33–5
Ahulu, S. 16
Allen, E. 152
Amador Moreno, C. 139, 140
American English 31, 57–8, 94, 139, 142–3
apostrophe 89–91, 172, 174–7
articles 77, 87–9, 127
Australia 141, 154–5, 167, 175, 176, 180
Australian Curriculum 2009 158–9
auxiliary *be* 61, 63
auxiliary *have* 62–3
auxiliary *do* 64–6
auxiliary verbs 35, 60–6

Bahasa Malaysia 78, 141
Banjo, A. 16
base form 30, 31, 134
Bernard, N. 154–5
Biber, D. 74
Bingle, B. 163
Bloomfield, L. 104–5, 124

BNC1994 13
BNClab 183
Bourhis, R. Y. 168
Brazil, D. 130, 132
British National Corpus 13
Bruthiaux, P. 170–1, 173
Bullokar, W. 11
Bushnell, A. 181
Bybee, J. 115, 133, 134

Cambridgeshire 136, 138
Canada 186
Canadian English 175, 179
Caribbean English 141, 179
Carter, R. 12, 38, 98, 128, 129, 144, 146, 153, 161, 167
case 150–1
Cheshire, J. 12
Chomsky, N. 105–10, 135, 154
chunks 133–4, 143
Clancy, B. 183
class conversion 58
clause 26–46, 68, 72, 84, 92, 117–18, 126–31, 148, 159
cleft sentence 52–3
closed systems 76–7, 117
cognitive grammar 110–13
coherence 50
cohesion 51
comparatives 6
competence 109, 115
complement 33, 94

compound 25, 91
concord 33–5
concordances 14
conditional 41–2
conjunctions, 40, 59, 91–3, 162, 172
Conrad, S. 74
context of situation 115–16
continuous aspect 61–2
coordinating conjunctions 40, 91–2
Cop, M. 176
corpus 12–15
Corrigan, K. 16, 140
countable nouns 56–8, 87
Croft, W. 114
Cruse, A. 114
Crystal, D. 187

declarative 30, 108
deep structure 110
defining relative clauses 44–5
definite article 7, 87–8
demonstratives 76, 84, 117
Dent, S. 171
deontic modality 66–8
Derewianka, B. 167
derived form 25
descriptive 9, 13
Deterding, D. 58
determiners 86–90
diachronic 102
dialect grammars 136–42
dialects 17
direct object 32, 36, 73
discourse grammar 50, 53
discourse marker 132–4
di-transitive verbs 36
Downing, A. 53
dummy *it* 80

East Midlands 10
Eastwood, J. 54
ellipsis 127–8, 141, 186
embedding 46
epistemic modality 66

etymology 10
Evans, V. 111
Everett, D. L. 8

face 67–9
Farr, F. 16
field 120
Finegan, E. 74
Firth, J. R. 115–6, 120
Francis, G. 135
French 30, 58, 64, 141, 150
frequency lists 13–14
Fries, C. C. 105, 153
fronted adverbials 35, 120, 164, 180–1

Gannon, S. 154
gender 58, 179
generic pronouns 78
German 150
get-passive 37, 38
Gove, M. 163, 165
Graffi, G. 121
grammar, definition 2
grammaticalization 133
Green, M. 111
Greenbaum, S. 19
Grice, E. 165
Gulliver's Travels 166
Gwynne, N. M. 163–5

Halliday, M. A. K. 29, 117–20, 122, 135–6, 155
Hancock, C. 154, 159
Harris, J. 140
Hatfield, H. 176
Hawking, S. 62
Hazen, K. 137
headers 128–30
hedging 66–7
Hickey, R. 140
Hopper, P. 115, 132
Horton, S. 163
Hudson, Rachel 142
Hudson, Richard 156
Hunston, S. 135

imperative 30, 32, 68
indefinite article 58, 87–9
indefinite pronouns 77, 81
Indian English 141
indirect object 32–3, 36, 150, 156
information focus 48
interjections 96–7
interrogative 30
interrogative pronouns 84
intransitive verbs 36
Irish English 139–41, 183, 186

Johansson, S. 74
Jones, C. 21
Jones, D. 146

Kamm, O. 165
Kingman Report 158, 160
Kirkpatrick, A. 144
Kolln, M. 154, 159

Landry, R. 168
Langacker, R. 110–14
Lange, C. 141, 144
Lange, D. 183
Latin 10–11, 23, 94, 149–54,
    160, 165
Leech, G. 19, 74, 123, 143
Leuckert, S. 141, 144
lexical verbs 27, 35, 185
like 76, 181–5
Limerick Corpus of spoken Irish
    English (LCIE) 140, 183
LINC (Language in the National
    Curriculum) 161
lingua franca 15, 144
linking expressions 50–2
Little, G. 175
lost generation 147–9
Lowth, R. 95, 101

main clause 38–9, 92, 172, 173
main verbs 60
Malaysia 125, 141
Malaysian English 58
Malinowski, B. 115

marked position 48
Mason, A. T. 152
Matthews, P. 105
McCarthy, M. J. 8, 53, 86, 98, 123,
    128, 129, 132, 144, 183
Milroy, J. 9, 137, 160
Milroy, L. 9, 137, 160
Milton, J. 11, 125
Mitchell, T. F. 116
modal verbs 41, 60, 66–70
mode 120
mood 30–1
moral panic 145–7, 154, 160
morphemes 23–5, 50
morphology 3, 116
Murphy, L. 143

National Curriculum for England
    2013 31, 162
negation 95
negative 32, 65, 68
negative adverbs 48, 95–6, 134
Neo-Firthians 115
Nesfield, J. C. 152–3
New Zealand 141, 176
Nigeria 1, 16
non-defining relative clauses 44–5
non-finite clauses 42
Norfolk 17, 138
Northern Ireland 17
nouns 55–60
number 55

O'Keeffe, A. 16, 139–40
O'Sullivan, J. 186
objects 32–33
Open American National Corpus
    142, 170
orthography 50, 116

Palmer, F. R. 116
Palmer, H. E. 105
passive voice 36–8, 63, 64,
    107–8, 163
past participle 37, 62, 138
past perfect 62–3

pattern grammar 135
Penhallurick, R. 138
perfect aspect 62–3
performance 109–10, 113
personal pronouns 77–9, 119
Peterson, E. 167, 183
phonology 50, 116
phrases 25–8
phrase structure 106–7, 108
Plain English Campaign 169
post-modifier 59–60
pragmatic markers 132
predicate 33, 106
pre-modifier 59–60
prepositions 44, 79, 93–5, 162
prescriptive 9
present participle 61
present perfect 62–3, 140, 162, 163
pronouns 77–86
proscriptive 9
psychological concord 34–5
punctuation 159, 162, 170–8

Quirk, R. 19, 127

Radford, A. 122
rank scale 117, 118
reciprocal pronouns 80
reflexive pronouns 77, 79, 179
register 13, 17–18
relative clauses 42–6, 82, 84
relative pronouns 43, 82–4
Report on Terminology 150–3
reported clauses 46
requests 69
response tokens 132
Revell, D. L. 179
Romaine, S. 183

Saussure, F. de 102–3, 105
Sawyer, W. 154
Schaffer, D. 9
Schiffrin, D. 132
Schmid, H.-J. 111, 114, 122
Schwyter, J. 12
Scollon, R. 187

Scollon, S. W. 187
Seely, J. 73
semantics 100, 105, 114
sentence 4, 38–40
sentential relative clauses 45
Shakespeare, W. 6, 11, 125
shared knowledge 88, 130
simple aspect 61–3
Sinclair, J. McH. 135
Singapore 15, 141
Singaporean English 58
Skinner, B. F. 109
South African English 16
Spanish 30, 47, 58, 65, 76, 96, 119
speaking and writing 123, 126, 160
Spoken BNC2014 13
standard grammar 10–12, 126, 160
Stern, N. 179
stranded prepositions 44, 94–5
structuralism 102–5, 153–4
subject 32–5, 36–7, 78, 119, 129
subjunctive 30–2
subordinate clauses 39–41, 92, 148
subordinators 40
substitute do 66
superlatives 6
surface structure 107, 110
Svartvik, J. 19
Swan, M. 21
Swedish 7, 61, 65, 141
Swift, J. 166
synchronic 102
syntax 3, 109, 114, 116, 158
systemic-functional grammar 119, 158

Tagliamonte, S. 142
tags 68
tails 128–9
Tamaredo, I. 141
tenor 120
Thompson, E. 184
Thompson, K. 146
Tomasello, M. 114
traditional grammar 149–153
transformational grammar 107–8, 122
transitive verbs 36, 130, 131

transitivity 36
Tristram Shandy 178
Trudgill, P. 17, 138, 187

UK National Curriculum 146
UK (United Kingdom) 12, 17, 146,
    155–66, 174, 177, 180
uncountable 56–8, 88, 168–9
Ungerer, F. 111, 114, 122
United States 17, 137, 153–4, 155,
    156, 159
universal grammar 7, 99
unmarked position 48, 49
usage-based grammar 114–5

Van Rooy, B. 16
varieties 16–17, 57, 65, 125, 139–141

verbs 28, 33, 36, 60–70, 142–3,
    162, 163

Wales 3, 136–8
Waller, D. 21
Walmsley, J. 156–7
Welsh 138–9, 141, 151, 156
Wikström, P. 184
word, definition 22–5
word classes 26, 55, 59, 131, 133
word-order 2–3, 7, 10, 30, 47–9, 71
World Englishes 15, 144

Yamaguchi, T. 58
Yorkshire 17

zero article 87–8

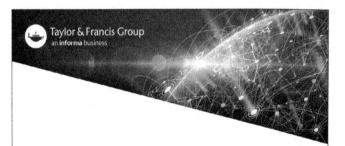